The Beginning
of Difference

Theodore Hiebert

The Beginning
of Difference

Discovering Identity in God's Diverse World

Abingdon Press
Nashville

THE BEGINNING OF DIFFERENCE:
Discovering Identity in God's Diverse World

Copyright © 2019 by Abingdon Press

All rights reserved.

Library of Congress Control Number: 2019949616

ISBN 978-1-5018-7102-3

19 20 21 22 23 24 25 26 27 28 29—10 9 8 7 6 5 4 3 2 1
MANUFACTURED IN THE UNITED STATES OF AMERICA

To Theo
and the next generation.
And to all the members of the McCormick community,
who are the real authors of this book.

Acknowledgments

This book was born at McCormick Theological Seminary, where I've taught the book of Genesis in a diverse community that shaped my learning, my teaching, my life, and the questions that inspired this book. So I acknowledge all the members of this community—students, staff, and faculty—who contributed in conscious and unconscious ways to the creation of this book. By discussing identity and difference with students in classes—The Tower of Babel and Cultural Diversity, or Biblical Perspectives on Multiculturalism—I learned new ways to think about our own differences and about what our scriptures have to say about them. The same exchange of ideas happened in conversations with faculty colleagues. They asked hard questions and provided important suggestions on various chapters of this book, which were discussed in monthly faculty scholarship lunches. Stephanie Crumpton, David Daniels, Leslie Diaz-Perez, Sarah Tanzer, David Watkins, and Reggie Williams all spoke with me individually about ideas I badly needed help with.

Several others have been truly crucial in making this project what it is. Thehil Russelliah Singh, a recent McCormick graduate and doctoral student in Old Testament, was a uniquely gifted conversation partner and ally. She's read each chapter, and she's helped me understand things about the language of kinship in Genesis, the experience of difference, and the world to which I'm writing that I'd otherwise have completely missed. Paul Franklyn, my editor at Abingdon, made this book happen. He's been my main cheerleader since I mentioned the project to him, a helpful conversation partner throughout, and one of the only people I know who can push things forward with both determination and grace. My wife, Paula, has been my partner in thinking and writing from the beginning. She has been with me all the way through this project too, listening constantly, talking about unformed and formed ideas, reading everything, adding clarity and precision, and making the whole book better and stronger.

And then there's Theo—who hasn't done anything at all but be born, in Brooklyn, at two o'clock in the morning, while this book was being written. His birth alone, and the new generation he represents, is inspiration for writing about the kind of lives we must live in a world of difference.

Introduction

The High Stakes of Difference

After growing up in small Mennonite communities in Kansas and California, and attending a Mennonite high school and then a Mennonite college (Fresno Pacific University), my own cultural identity was a given and hardly necessary to think about. Cultural difference, for practical purposes, was a distant reality. My first real encounter with cultural difference came when I left this small Mennonite world in the United States to join the Teachers Abroad Program of the Mennonite Central Committee and was assigned to teach English at Numan Teachers College in North Eastern Nigeria. I was twenty-one years old. I cannot fully explain how completely different this world was and how it felt to me. It was so different that in the first weeks and months, I feared not surviving the three-year term of my assignment.

Before long, I learned several important lessons. I learned what it was like to be a minority in a culture where I and my cultural identity was not the norm. I learned that, though I went to Nigeria as an idealistic, service-minded college graduate intending to help the world, I would not survive on my own. I would survive the teaching term I had signed up for only through the goodwill and hospitality of the Nigerian community where I lived and taught. I also learned that, though a minority and though utterly dependent on my Nigerian hosts and friends, I was still a privileged minority. I was a white American who represented in the minds of many of my Nigerian students all the resources and opportunities they sought.

I learned another crucial thing. I learned about the imposition of Western Christian cultural norms on the members of the Bachama people in and around Numan who had become Christians and who followed a traditional Western order of worship in the Danish Lutheran church in the middle of town. For the first time, I began to think about cultural and religious differences, about the challenges to the ethnic identity of the Bachama people posed by the influx of Western missionaries with their different cultural norms. I observed the damage to the dignity of a people such an imposition of other foreign cultural norms can inflict. In all this, the Nigerian author Chinua Achebe was my best teacher. In *Things Fall Apart*, which I taught to my high school English class, he told the true story of the positive and negative effects of Western Christianity moving into South Eastern Nigeria.

This book about difference began there, in Numan, Nigeria. But this book actually came into being as it now exists at McCormick Theological Seminary in the Hyde Park neighborhood of South Chicago, where I have taught the Hebrew scriptures for more than twenty years. Before finding my home at McCormick, I taught in three different American cultures: the Swedish Lutheran culture at Gustavus Adolphus College in St. Peter, Minnesota; the Cajun culture at Louisiana State University in Baton Rouge; and the New England culture at Harvard Divinity School. And with my family I lived for a year in Jerusalem, the sacred center of Judaism, Christianity, and Islam. Jerusalem is also the epicenter of conflict among these religious traditions. But this book was really conceived and shaped at McCormick.

McCormick is a small, very diverse religious community that is trying every day to find ways to live with difference in a healthy and positive way and to build a model of what this might look like. During most of the twenty-plus years I have taught at

McCormick, it has been a community without a cultural majority. The school includes students who are African-American, Asian-American, Columbian, Egyptian, European-American, Indian, Indian-American, Kenyan, Korean, Latinx, Nicaraguan, Puerto Rican, and Taiwanese. This list is not yet a complete accounting of all those who have been part of our community. We are a community that also comes from different sectors of the church: Baptist, Catholic, Church of God in Christ, Mennonite, Methodist, Pentecostal, Presbyterian (which founded McCormick), United Church of Christ, and many others. We are at least as diverse a cultural community as the community gathered in Jerusalem when the church was born at Pentecost.

In such a community, questions of identity and difference are continually in the air. While living with others who are different from myself, how do I discover, develop, articulate, and express my own identity? Who am I in relation to others, and how can I become my own authentic self? How do I develop relationships with my neighbors who are different from me? How do we learn to understand and communicate with each other across our differences? How do we honor and respect each other's voices equally and equitably? How do we create institutional structures that open space for all and do not privilege some over others? How do we model a healthy respect for identity and difference? This work of trying to figure out how to live together affects everything. It affects how we recruit students, how we organize community activities, how we plan worship, how we talk in the hallways, how we think about the church in the world, how we conceptualize ministry itself, how we structure our curriculum, and how we teach. It affects how my students read the Bible and how I teach it.

The questions we ask at McCormick about identity and difference are simply particular versions of the questions we all ask as citizens of the world and of any particular country in it. Countries around the world have recently elected more nationalist and populist leaders who hold inward-looking and isolationist views and who are more suspicious of other nations, international cooperation, and global agreements. Internally, nations on all continents are composed themselves of multiple cultural communities that often cooperate but that also can provoke intense ethnic conflicts and violence within. Difference can be a source of vast enrichment and growth—or a reason for hate, exclusion, discrimination, and violence. Difference can be a weapon to divide and conquer. The stakes of difference are high.

The United States, through constant immigration, has emerged as one of the most diverse countries on earth. The opportunities and the challenges this diversity engenders are immense. The Obama administration and the Trump presidency that followed made it clear that racial discrimination and white privilege remain deeply seated and virulent. The growing pride and powerful voices from all ethnicities in the US have awakened consciousness and opened the door for new dialogues and for new opportunities. The conversation today about identity and difference is as energetic, lively, significant, and crucial for the future as it has ever been. In the United States, it is inspired in great part by the voices of marginalized communities that are challenging the dominant role that one particular culture—white culture made up of immigrants from Europe—has held in American society as the norm by which others are measured and by which all others are allowed or not allowed access to power and privilege.

This summary is, of course, a vast oversimplification, since merely a generation ago a friend of my Irish in-laws, from one of these white European countries, was told not to apply for a banking job in Providence, Rhode Island, because she was Irish and Catholic. My German Mennonite ancestor immigrants from Europe faced the same hostility when they arrived in New York at the end of the nineteenth century on their way to the Midwest. But the privileging of white culture has been deeply, dangerously true in America throughout its history. Immigrants from Europe have been responsible for the decimation of Native Americans.

Immigrants from Europe enslaved African-Americans and built into American society the deep racism that continues to exist in the US today. This history and the modern expressions of it are the primary context for the conversation about difference and the struggle for identity and equality in America's diverse society. This heritage drives the immigration debate, and it continues to determine the opportunities for dignity, equality, and well-being among all people in America today.

I believe firmly, as do the other members of the McCormick community in Chicago where this book was born, that our deepest values determine our actions. And for this community and many communities where Christianity, Judaism, or Islam have taken root, biblical texts influence those core values. That is why I am writing this book. The book of Genesis is the biblical book I've taught and studied the most during my time at McCormick. My questions about Genesis, because of engaging with McCormick's diverse community, have increasingly focused on the topics of identity and difference. Does our scripture, particularly the Bible's first and hugely influential book—the book whose stories have embedded themselves so deeply in minds and cultures around the world—speak to the topics of identity and difference? If Genesis does, does it speak helpfully from the beginning about these topics or not? Do the attitudes toward difference in Genesis feed into our fears about difference or do they give us creative ways of flourishing equitably within it? What kind of conversation partner is the book of Genesis for finding ways of affirming both our own identities and the different identities of others in our various social settings in the US and in the world today?

Identity and Difference

This book is about cultural identity and difference and the attitudes toward them, so I want to be clear about how I am using the language of culture in this book. "Culture," as cultural anthropologists describe it, is made up of all the aspects that give shape to our social lives and give us a particular group identity: ancestry, history, language, living space, arts, religion, values, institutions, rituals, laws, customs, clothing, food. An "ethnic group" is a community that shares a common cultural tradition that is distinctive to itself and different from others with their own specific traditions.[1] So when I speak of "ethnicity" or "ethnic identity," I am referring to membership and belonging in such a group with a common and distinctive set of cultural traditions. In this book, therefore, the phrases "cultural identity" and "ethnic identity" are for all practical purposes synonymous. Likewise, "cultural difference" and "ethnic difference" both refer to groups with another set of distinctive shared traditions. As we will see, language, land, and descent (ancestry) are the three primary markers of ethnic identity and difference we will encounter in the narratives of Genesis.

Scholars across disciplines now agree that ethnicity or ethnic identity is a social construction. It is created within a community itself over time to express its definition of itself and its sense of solidarity. Because of this, ethnic identity is flexible and fluid, and it can change as social circumstances change. Ethnicity or ethnic identity is not biologically innate. It is not genetically determined, natural, inherent, and unchangeable. Members of ethnic groups both in antiquity and today often do make the claim that they are connected by common ancestry and by blood and that they are defined, in fact, biologically. They do this to deepen their sense of unity. Members of ethnic groups also claim this of others, often to stereotype, mistreat, and victimize them. Although families and extended families within ethnic groups share genetic connections, the overall claims of identity within an ethnic group go far beyond this and are essential social definitions and claims.

---

1. Conrad Phillip Kottak, *Cultural Anthropology*, 6th ed. (New York: McGraw-Hill, 1994), 39, 52.

In popular American thinking and conversation, the word "race" is closely associated with ethnicity, so that, for example, the term "racial-ethnic" is used by some to describe cultural identities. Using this word as another designation of ethnicity, however, usually carries with it a biological definition of ethnicity, a definition that proves inaccurate and even dangerous. A modern English dictionary, such as the *American Heritage Dictionary*, contains just such a definition of "race": a "population distinguished as a more or less distinct group by genetically transmitted physical characteristics." Cultural anthropologists, in fact, reserve the term "race" for ethnic groups *assumed* to have a biological basis.[2] Scholars now agree that such biological claims are in fact fictive social claims of commonality that cannot be established by science. In order to avoid the implication that ethnic identity is, in fact, genetically determined, I prefer using the terms "ethnic" and "cultural identity" over racial identity in this book.

At the same time, I recognize the complexity of this issue and the impossibility of clearly differentiating ethnic and racial claims as I defined them above. When the authors of Genesis use the language of kinship to define their own ethnic identity, and their relationship to other ethnicities as well, they are clearly making biological claims of common ancestry, descent, and relatedness. This grows out of actual genetic relations at the family level, though even there servants and immigrants gain family membership through fictive kinship. At the level of village, tribe, and people—that is, the people of Israel—kinship becomes entirely fictive and a social construction of the society known as Israel. In the contemporary world, claims of biological and social unity are also intertwined, so that ethnicity and race are hard to distinguish. To clarify for purposes of this book, when I use the term "race," primarily in more contemporary contexts, I mean it itself to be a socially constructed concept, a concept primarily constructed by America's white culture to disadvantage peoples of color.

---

2. Kottak, *Cultural Anthropology*, 52.

As we noted, the primary markers of ethnic identity and difference in the book of Genesis are language, land, and descent. This means that two of the most common markers of cultural difference in the contemporary world are essentially absent in Genesis. The most surprising one is religion. This is especially remarkable, since in much of the Bible, religion is the crucial marker of identity and difference. In Deuteronomy and its related traditions, for example, worshipping the LORD (Yahweh) to the exclusion of other gods signals the core identity of the true Israelite and the only path toward well-being and flourishing as a distinctive people and culture (Deut 5:7; 6:12-15; 7:1-4). The prophets also weigh in repeatedly against idolatry, the worship of other deities, in particular, the Canaanite god Baal (Isa 41:21-29; Jer 2:20-23; Hos 4:12-19). In the Christian scriptures, of course, joining the Jesus movement entirely defines Christian communities. In Genesis, however, as we will see, difference is not defined by religious affiliation. The characters who are part of the lineage of Israel and those who are part of other lineages all communicate with and relate to a single God.

The other common marker of difference in the contemporary world, yet absent in Genesis, is distinguishing peoples and ethnicities by skin color. It's accurate to say that the genealogies in Genesis have been interpreted by American readers as dividing white and black "races," and they have been used virulently in American history to defend white superiority and to support the enslavement and segregation of black peoples. But these claims are completely false interpretations of Genesis, whose authors never used skin color as an ethnic distinction or as a characteristic in defining difference. While these two aspects of contemporary cultural differentiation are absent in Genesis, I intend that the biblical engagement with identity and difference in Genesis will be useful for negotiating difference in these crucial contemporary ways as well. I hope that the affirmation of unique identities and the embrace of difference that we will see expressed by Genesis's authors will be a value we can translate into an American culture so divided by differences based on religion and skin color.

To conclude these words on the language of identity and difference, consider the use of the term "difference" in the title of this book. In a lecture on conceptualizing and engaging difference called "Differential Equations: On Constructing the 'Other,'" University of Chicago professor Jonathan Z. Smith outlines three fundamental ways in which individuals and groups have viewed others as different from themselves, and he discusses the consequences of these views.[3] The first two ways use real cultural or physical distinctions to identify differences. According to one, the presence or absence of one cultural trait stands in for the whole, so that, for example, the ancient Sumerians described the Amorites as those who "do not know barley," that is, those who are non-agrarian and nomadic. Similarly, modern Americans use a single physical characteristic like skin color, white or black or brown or yellow or red, to identify a different group. According to Smith's second way of distinguishing others, the distance from the center of one's world defines difference, where those nearest are most similar and those distant are most different. The ancient Greeks considered the Indians the strangest of all peoples because they were at the farthest reaches of Alexander the Great's conquests. Each of these two ways of viewing difference is highly ambivalent, according to Smith, because each also recognizes a deep connection or continuity between oneself and others that allows one to make such differentiations.

A third way of viewing difference, however, blocks connection of any kind. This is a more recent approach in Smith's opinion, which describes difference in terms of intelligibility. According to this view, the "Other" possesses a completely different mentality that is entirely unintelligible and forever remains so. While this view of difference was not held in antiquity, it has become a

---

3. Jonathan Z. Smith, "Differential Equations: On Constructing the 'Other'" (Thirteenth Annual University Lecture in Religion, Arizona State University, Tempe, AZ, March 5, 1992).

powerful perspective today. It is at play when contemporary scholars or writers depict ancient cultures, or more traditional contemporary cultures, as "primitive," "prehistoric," or "irrational." They will never be understood. It is this notion of those who are different as completely unintelligible that the language of "Other" has been designed to express. It is a language that blocks engagement of any kind, unlike language of difference, which recognizes an underlying connection between self and others. Consider how Smith expresses it:

> It must be insisted that the language of the "other" always invites misunderstanding, suggesting, as it does, an ontological cleavage rather than an anthropological distinction. Much better is the language of "difference," which is as relational and relative a terminology as the "other" is absolute. "Otherness" blocks language and conception; "difference" invites negotiation and intellection. For "difference" is an active term—ultimately a verbal form, *differre*, "to carry apart"—suggesting the separation out of what, from another vantage point, might be seen as the "same." By contrast, "other" has no verbal form, except, perhaps, "alienate," which, tellingly, most often appears in the passive voice. Viewed in this light, difference is the more interesting phenomenon which has not received the attention it merits.[4]

This is a nearly perfect definition of the understanding of difference in the book of Genesis, and it is the meaning I intend in the title of this book. In Genesis, difference is an active concept suggesting the separation out of what, from another vantage point, might be seen as the same. This understanding is articulated in Genesis, as we will see, primarily by the use of kinship language for identity and difference. Kinship language clearly draws definite distinctions between the different lineages and members of a family, but it always locates those distinctions within a family tree that claims common descent. In such a conception of the world, difference is always described as relational.

---

4. Smith, "Differential Equations," 10.

By writing on ethnic identity and difference, I will not analyze other kinds of difference, for example, differences of gender and sexuality. Gender identity and difference are, of course, deeply imbedded in the narratives of Genesis, where some texts legitimate the patriarchal structure of biblical society, while others undermine it. Feminist criticism has introduced a broad and ongoing conversation about this kind of difference, which I will not be able to deal with substantively here. Further, the issue of sexual orientation, which is so divisive in religious communities today, is by and large absent from the Genesis narratives, though the story of Sodom and Gomorrah has been used incorrectly to support homophobia in many circles. While such other important differences as these are beyond the scope of this book, I hope, again, that the affirmation of identity and the embrace of difference imbedded in the values of Genesis might be values that could be brought to bear on other differences we encounter in society today.

Identity and Difference in the Bible

The Bible is hardly the first place people go to look for constructive models of identity and of engaging difference. In fact, many think first of the Bible as a book filled with the most difficult and disastrous images of difference: unending wars, fierce intolerance of other peoples, and even mass extermination of other cultures—and all this under God's direction and command. When people find out I teach the Bible, sometimes their first question is: "What do you do about all the wars?" This is a very legitimate question, even though it's not the place I'd want to start a conversation about the Bible. It's a popular perception, but it's based on real biblical texts and ideas.

The book of Deuteronomy, to cite one example, draws a sharp distinction between Israel and others. It prohibits Israel from having any interaction with its neighbors or adopting any of their practices. Moses commands Israel to make no agreements with the people of the land they are to enter, and not to intermarry with them. He commands Israel not to worship their gods but also to destroy their holy places and tear down their sanctuaries. Moses commands, in fact, the worst of all possible actions: the mass extermination of these peoples. Failure to take this antagonistic and destructive stance toward its neighbors will result, says Moses, in God destroying the Israelites themselves (Deut 7:1-6). One could add to this example the prophetic oracles against the nations that portray God destroying neighboring nations completely (e.g., Isa 13–19). However one tries to contextualize these attitudes in light of the ancient cultural and political world Israel inhabited, they remain fundamentally alarming and perilous teachings.

A version of this suspicion of the Bible as a resource for thinking about identity and difference is the sense in Christian communities that their Old Testament as a whole really has nothing useful at all to say about difference, but that their New Testament can give them important guidance. When I've asked members of Christian congregations whether they think the Bible contains any helpful resources for thinking about cultural identity and difference, they tend to look straight to the New Testament and cite the stories about the good Samaritan or Jesus's teaching to "love your neighbor," which, by the way, is a direct quotation from Leviticus 19:18. When pushed about their Old Testament, they may cite Ruth, Rahab, or texts about the sojourner, but they think of these as anomalies. Indeed, Christians tend to have a very binary view of the Bible. They carry with them the idea that the Old Testament contains a nationalistic, ethnocentric, Israelite view of the world, while the New Testament and Christianity preach a universal, ethnic-free Christianity. This is a false stereotype we will challenge in the chapter on Pentecost.[5]

---

5. Eric D. Barreto, "Negotiating Difference: Theology and Ethnicity in the Acts of the Apostles," *Word & World* 31, no. 2 (Spring 2011): 130–31.

As a matter of fact, the Bible contains a wide spectrum of very different perspectives on identity and on engaging others who are different, some, including the book of Genesis, the direct opposite of the antagonistic views of the author of Deuteronomy. The Bible is essentially a library made up of a collection of writings composed over a thousand-year period in many different times and social contexts. We might expect it, therefore, to contain a wide range of beliefs, opinions, and attitudes about difference. In a single book like this one, this whole range of viewpoints is impossible to describe adequately. Our aim in this book is to explore in depth the viewpoints present in one crucial and influential part of the Bible, the book of Genesis.

Identity and Difference in Genesis

The book of Genesis is particularly important for investigating the Bible's views about difference. One reason for this is its character as a collection of origin stories. Origin stories are foundational for the societies who tell them. Origin stories, while about the very beginnings of a people, are not really about the past. They are about the present. By describing their origins, a society describes who it is in the present. Origin stories answer the questions: Who are we? Why are we this way? How did we get to be the way we are? They are, therefore, defining stories, narratives that define the identity of the people telling them. They contain founding statements about the core aspects of their teller's identity. They define the most elemental parts of the ethnic and cultural character of the people who tell them. Origin stories, by virtue of their defining character, carry in them the deepest values of the culture from which they come. So, by reading the book of Genesis, we can expect to encounter the very bedrock views of the Bible's understanding of identity and difference. In its stories about the beginning of difference, its authors reveal their deepest values.

Another important reason for exploring the viewpoints in Genesis about identity and difference is the book's resilience and lasting power. Genesis is one of the most influential books in the Bible. Its stories are some of the most well-known stories, and they live in the minds and hearts of all those who are heirs of this scripture, even though they may no longer be practicing participants in religious communities. The stories of Genesis have become iconic in all the cultures around the world in which Judaism, Christianity, or Islam have taken root. They remain part of the modern consciousness, and they continue to influence how people think and act. In this regard, the stories in Genesis are not just part of an archaic scriptural tradition. They have become part of the modern world, and they continue to make it what it is.

Finally—and this is really one of the most important reasons for this book—Genesis's readers and interpreters have over the years come to *misunderstand* its values toward identity and difference in some very basic ways. Specifically, Genesis's interpreters have followed a trajectory, begun very early in the history of interpretation, which has portrayed the book in more and more exclusivist terms. In this history, Genesis's interpreters have constructed a growing binary viewpoint, dividing Israel in sharper and sharper ways from others. And they have viewed others in more and more negative terms, so that difference has come to be understood in increasingly fearful and dangerous terms. We will embark on a journey in this book to rediscover the much more inclusivist views of Genesis's authors, which have become obscured over time. And we will do so in order to retrieve a conversation partner that can help us think more generously about difference today.

In each of the four chapters of this book, we examine a key text or texts in Genesis, together with one in the Acts of the Apostles, that continue to influence how people think about identity and difference today. In each case, we will challenge the exclusivist trajectory of interpretation that governed interpreters in the past, and we will recover a more inclusivist reading that was obscured by this history of interpretation, a reading that is embedded in the text itself and that is intended by its authors. In chapter 1, "Difference Begins at Babel," we will take a fresh look at one of the most famous stories in all Western literature, the story of the Tower of Babel (Gen 11:1-9). This is the Bible's classic explanation of the world's cultural differences. We will consider the implications of the historical trajectory of interpretation, in which the construction of ethnic identity is considered arrogant and in which the beginning of difference is viewed as God's punishment on the world, a curse humans must bear. We will recover the author's constructive view of the deep human drive for ethnic identity and his view of God's plan to create a world of difference, a profusion of ethnic identities and cultures.

In chapter 2, "Noah's Descendants: Biblical Writers Choose Their Family," we will examine Genesis's authors' understanding of their own ethnic identity in relationship to others. We will consider the implications of the interpretive trajectory in which Israel's family is limited to the descendants of Abraham, and we will recover the authors' view that they and their ethnic culture are in fact members of Noah's descendants, and that they are therefore related to the entire human family.

In chapter 3, "Biblical Peoples Live with Difference," we will reread stories in Genesis of tension, conflict, negotiation, resolution, hospitality, alliance, and trust to discover biblical values toward living with difference. We will reexamine a more exclusivist reading of these narratives that privilege Israel alone, and consider the authors' own sense of Israel's acceptance of and respect for the place of others in their world.

In chapter 4, "Pentecost: The First Christians Embrace Difference," we will move into the world of early Christianity in order to examine the way in which Luke, the author of the Pentecost narrative, adapted the story of Babel to write a charter for the early church. We will see that his aim was not to reverse the difference created at Babel, as so many interpreters have claimed, but to build upon that diversity. He wanted to show that the church's diversity would mirror the world's diversity. In this way, we will explore the reverberations of the story of Babel, the Bible's classic story of difference, in Christian thought, and its continued influence among successive generations who lived in a world of difference.

The Authors of Genesis

To study Genesis authentically, we take into consideration its authors and their historical and social contexts. This is not easy. They do not identify themselves in the pages of their work, as do, for example, the prophets, whose signatures appear at the beginning of their collected speeches. The early interpreters of Genesis gave Moses credit for writing it, because he wrote down the instructions from God at Mount Sinai (Deut 31:9, 24-26), though he is nowhere identified in the Bible as the author of Genesis. For over five hundred years, scholars have called attention to incongruities and inconsistences that make Mosaic authorship highly unlikely, and this led to a long and continuing debate about who the author or authors might actually be, when they might have lived, and what their social settings might have looked like. There has never been complete consensus.

In the nineteenth and twentieth centuries, a view of authorship emerged that, while still debated, became widespread and has many adherents today, of which I am one. According to this view, Genesis contains a collection of the traditions about Israel's past from three different settings or individuals. These individuals are almost certainly preservers of traditions of their past that they themselves did not create or invent. So they are not authors or writers in the modern sense, who created new accounts that had not existed before. Yet their traditions are so unique and distinct in terms of their vocabulary, style, and perspective that we can recognize them as unique voices, preserving unique viewpoints about their world and about their past. So, though they are not authors in the modern sense, I often use this word for them in order to indicate the unified and unique way of thinking possessed by each.

The earliest author in the book of Genesis is the Storyteller. He is the author of the story of Babel discussed in chapter 1, of most of the traditions of Israel's earliest history analyzed in chapter 2, and of many of the stories of Israel's ancestors interacting with their neighbors examined in chapter 3. Scholars have called him the Yahwist, because one of his most distinctive features is to refer to God by Israel's proper name for God, Yahweh, from the very beginning of time. His traditions have the flavor of ancient epic narratives reflecting the lives of quintessential Israelites, who were Mediterranean highland farmers. If I were to characterize him, I would call him one in a line of ancient epic singers of traditions, traditions he himself had learned and that he passed down to the next generation. So I call him the Storyteller. When his traditions came to be written down in the form we now possess, they were written down by him or a scribe during the Davidic monarchy. They explain the rise of David's tribe of Judah to prominence and its role in uniting the tribes of Israel, represented in Genesis by the sons of Jacob/Israel, a topic we will return to in chapter 3.

A second author of Genesis is the Priest. He is called the Priestly Writer by scholars, who have noticed that his traditions can be distinguished from the Storyteller's by his special interest in religious and ritual matters, and by his use of the common word for God, Elohim. For example, the Priest's creation narrative in Genesis 1:1–2:4a concludes with the institution of the Sabbath. He also has a more formal style and has an accountant's interest in numbers: days, months, years, ages. He has a Priest's obsession with proper orders and records. He is responsible, for example, for the great genealogy in Genesis 10, which provides an alternative account of the spread of the world's cultures to the Storyteller's account of Babel in Genesis 11. Scholars have often dated him later than the Yahwist, even to the post-exilic period after the end of the Davidic monarchy, and this is likely, but his traditions are certainly older in origin. In my judgment, as some others hold, he is not only the preserver of priestly traditions but also the figure who combined his traditions with the Storyteller's, and also with a third writer's traditions, in order to compile the books of Genesis, Exodus, Leviticus, and Numbers as we have them today.

This third writer provides historical traditions that only begin in Genesis 20. So his traditions have not been as prominent as the Storyteller's and the Priest's, and we will encounter this writer only in chapter 3. But he will be very important there, through his accounts of Israel's ancestors' relationships with the ancestors of other peoples. He preserves epic traditions that parallel the Story-teller's in many ways, and so he is kind of a second storyteller with a slightly different perspective. He is more interested in the morality of ancestral behavior, in prophetic themes and concepts, in Northern Israelite tribes and places, and he has a style all his own. Because he also uses the word *Elohim* for Israel's deity, scholars call him the Elohist. I have called him the Northern Storyteller, to distinguish him from the Storyteller related to the Davidic monarchy in the South.

Modern readers may well raise questions about the historical veracity of these narratives in Genesis. Contemporary discoveries, scientific advances, and historical investigations have posed legitimate questions about how historical these ancient stories of creation, long-lived ancestors, a global flood and the survival of a single family, and the existence and movements of Israel's ancestors actually are. For the purposes of this book, making a decision about the historical reliability of these accounts is not crucial. We are interested here in the values about identity and difference embedded in these narratives; that is, we are interested in the ideas and perspectives on difference their authors hold, regardless of the historicity of their stories. I believe these stories incorporate some actual historical realities from antiquity, in particular, the emergence of Israel in antiquity as a tribal kingdom tracing itself back to Jacob/Israel, Noah, and Adam. But I do not believe we can corroborate the details of the figures and events in these stories. We can, however, rely on the fact that these stories reflected the historical and cultural world of their authors, the Storyteller, the Northern Storyteller, and the Priest. And I, personally, think the authors believed these stories happened just as they told them.

Looking Ahead

This is a radical book. It's radical because it contains interpretations of the first book of the Bible, the book of Genesis, that are entirely new and different. It challenges some of the oldest and most widely accepted ways of reading Genesis, ways that we've simply accepted as truth and that have become part of our lives and part of the way we view the world. This book claims that some of these accepted ways of reading Genesis are problematic for living in the world, if not dysfunctional and downright dangerous. This book is a challenge to some of our most comfortable and unquestioned ideas—especially when it comes to difference and our attitude toward it. This book is radical because it claims that the writers of Genesis have something new to tell us about difference. The stories of Genesis that we've taken to be great problems for engaging difference actually treat difference with wisdom, respect, and generosity.

But this is also a very conservative book, not in the modern political definition of that term, but in the sense that it seeks to go back and recover the original views and values of biblical texts. It seeks above all to listen to what the writers of Genesis actually said. It aims to go back to the sources themselves and recover the original voices of scripture. It aims to penetrate behind the lenses we've acquired in the years since the stories of Genesis were written, lenses that have redirected the meaning of these texts for centuries. One of the great contributions of James Kugel's study of biblical interpretation is his insight and his demonstration of the fact that the Bible we think we know is not the Bible on the page but the Bible of its interpreters, the Bible they have put in our minds.[6] The aim of this book is conservative. It seeks to hear as clearly as possible the original voices of the authors of Genesis and to see what sense we might make of them when dealing with difference today.

This is also a contemporary book. The struggle for identity and the encounter with difference is as old as humankind. The writers of Genesis struggled just as we do to articulate and preserve their own identity and to negotiate constructively a world of difference. And that experience had all the pitfalls, challenges, and opportunities for them that it does for us. As we reexamine Genesis's writers' values about identity and difference in their world, they force us to reexamine our own values about identity and difference in our world as well. In this book I want to show that the authors of Genesis did so with a more constructive and positive attitude than we have recognized. And by doing this I want to open up a more productive and useful conversation about identity and difference between all of us in the world today, a conversation that leads to actions that dismantle structures of cultural privilege and that grant dignity and opportunity to all.

---

6. James L. Kugel, *The Bible as It Was* (Cambridge, MA: Harvard University Press, 1997), 1–49.

Chapter 1

Difference Begins
at Babel

*Teach her about difference. Make difference ordinary. Make difference normal.
Teach her not to attach value to difference. And the reason for this is not to be
fair or nice, but merely to be human and practical. Because difference is the
reality of our world. And by teaching her about difference, you are
equipping her to survive in a diverse world.*

—Chimamanda Ngozi Adichie's fifteenth suggestion to her friend in
Dear Ijeawele, or A Feminist Manifesto in Fifteen Suggestions[1]

C himamanda Adichie made this suggestion about living
with difference to her friend Ijeawele, who asked Adichie
for advice about raising her daughter in today's world.
Yet Adichie's view of difference is an almost perfect description of
the message about difference in the ancient story of Babel in Genesis 11, written nearly three thousand years ago. The ancient Storyteller who told the Babel story was also teaching about difference.
And he used this story to explain his own culture's wisdom about
it: that difference was normal; that it was a reality of our world.
Even more, that difference was God's intention for the world. Un-
fortunately, we've been taught to read the Bible's story of Babel as
a story teaching that difference is dangerous.

---

1. Chimamanda Ngozi Adichie, *Dear Ijeawele, or A Feminist Manifesto in Fifteen Suggestions* (New York: Knopf, 2017), 61.

Chapter 1

A Troubling Legacy

The acclaimed movie *Babel*, winner of the Golden Globe Award for Best Motion Picture in 2006, provides a striking example of how we understand the biblical story of Babel today. Written by Guillermo Arriaga and directed by Alejandro González Iñárritu, *Babel* stars Gael García Bernal, Kōji Yakusho, Cate Blanchett, and Brad Pitt, who, in the movie's trailer, reads these words *adapted* from Genesis 11:

> In the beginning, all the Lord's people from all parts of the world spoke one language. Nothing they proposed was impossible for them. . . . But hearing what the spirit of man could accomplish, the Lord said, Let us go down and confuse their language so that they may not understand one another's speech.

As Brad Pitt reads from Genesis 11, the movie's trailer projects vivid and troubling images of ethnic tension, misunderstanding, conflict, and violence in Morocco, Japan, and at the Mexico-US border. We are obviously to understand that the cultural confusion and strife we're watching, and the painful experience of difference it portrays, originated as a human trait in the Bible's story of Babel, as told in the book of Genesis.

Because the story of Babel is widely known, this negative understanding of it continues to reinforce our thinking about difference as dangerous. This chapter reexamines the story of Babel. I intend to show how readers over the centuries have imposed this negative perception on top of the story. We will learn how the story of Babel actually sees difference as normal, as part of the reality of our world, and from the biblical point of view, as God's intention for society. We will uncover how and why we've been influenced to read this story so differently, as if difference were a problem we've inherited from the beginning of time and a threat to our living together in the world. By recovering this story's more generous view of difference, I hope to challenge pessimistic views about difference that consider it a threat and open up to its readers more helpful and positive ways of living with difference today.

I've frequently asked members of religious congregations in the Chicago area and members of classes I've taught at McCormick Theological Seminary to write out the story of the Tower of Babel as they remember it. Here is an example from a McCormick class.

> Human beings gathered together in one place and decided to be one people with one language to build a tower all the way up to heaven. God saw what they were doing and said, "If they are one people with one language they will be as powerful as God," so God confused their languages so that they couldn't understand one another, and dispersed them over the face of the earth, and so they called the place Babel, because there, God confused their languages.

Embedded in this memory of the story is the view that the people of Babel built their tower to reach all the way up to heaven and to become just as powerful as God. God tried to restrain their arrogant ambition to be like God by spreading confusion among people by giving them different languages and different lands.

This student's memory of the story of Babel, with few variations, was shared by everyone in the class. The class was very diverse. It included students who were African-American, European-American, Indian-American, Japanese-American, Kenyan, Korean, and Latinx. This way of reading the story is not a local or culturally specific one. It is widespread across the United States and around the world. We are taught to read the story this way. John Milton inscribed this reading in Western literature when he retold the story of Babel in his great literary epic *Paradise Lost*, and all children's Bible storybooks today interpret the story in just this way. Babel has become synonymous with confusion. It symbolizes the view that difference is an obstacle to living together and a problem to be overcome.

We may call this interpretation of the Tower of Babel the "pride and punishment" reading of the story. Out of pride, the people build a tower to assert their autonomy, attack heaven, and challenge God. "Nothing they proposed was impossible for them," narrates Brad Pitt in *Babel*'s trailer. "They will be as powerful as God," says our student at McCormick. God punishes their arrogance by ending the building project, confusing the peoples' languages, and scattering the people across the world. This way of reading the story makes difference a punishment. It's God's penalty for human pride and God's way to restrain any further outbreaks of it. Difference becomes a disturbing fact and the reason for confusion and conflict among people. And since the story of Babel is the Bible's primary account of the beginning of difference, we have learned to connect the Bible itself to this dismal view of difference.

We can trace this "pride and punishment" reading of the Tower of Babel, with its negative view of difference, all the way back to the first record we have of anyone reading and interpreting this story. This reader and writer is the author of *Jubilees*, a priest in approximately 200 BCE who held a very negative view of other nations, believing them impure and destined for destruction. He retells the story by adding details not found in the biblical story, which turn it into the story of pride and punishment that people remember: the people are "evil with perverse counsel," they construct the tower to "go up in it into heaven," and, at the end, God sends "a great wind upon the tower and overthrew it on the earth." None of these details is in the story itself in the book of Genesis, but this negative view of the story and of the cultural difference that it explains became the norm.

Interpreters of the story of Babel for the past two thousand years followed the lead of *Jubilees*. They too read the story as a story of pride with difference as its punishment. This is true of Jewish interpreters, from the first-century historian Flavius Josephus to the late twentieth- and early twenty-first-century biblical scholar Nahum Sarna. It is just as true of Christian interpreters, from the late fourth- and early fifth-century theologian Augustine of Hippo, through the Protestant Reformers Martin Luther and John Calvin, to the twentieth-century biblical scholar Gerhard von Rad. Babel appears in book titles such as *Ethics after Babel* and *Biblical Authority after Babel* to describe the diversity of approaches in modern ethics or the diversity of modern interpretive approaches to the Bible as a distressing difficulty to be resolved.

This is a serious matter. Listen to the great Protestant reformer Martin Luther's response to the story of Babel:

> A horrible punishment followed, which, in my estimation, brought greater harm to the human race than the Flood itself...Where the languages differ, there not only no commerce develops, but hatred arises in the heart against that nation whose language you do not understand...Consequently, you can call it the seedbed of all evils.

Put succinctly: Difference is worse than death! If the difference introduced at Babel is the "seedbed of all evils," worse even than the universal death and destruction of the worldwide flood itself, then we all begin thinking about difference dangerously. We begin with the idea that the difference we live with every day is a terrible curse to be borne, an impossible problem to be surmounted, a danger to us all.

Rereading the Story of Babel

As we reexamine the story in this chapter, in its explicit claims and in all its concrete details, the story says nothing about pride and punishment and nothing about difference as the penalty for human sin. The story of Babel is really a straightforward and positive story about cultural identity and cultural difference. It presents the formation of cultural identity as a normal and admirable human activity, and it views cultural difference not as God's punishment on the world but as the way God intended the world to be. Along the way, we will see how we got off on the wrong track in our reading of this story and how we came to regard difference as a punishment to bear. Our aim is to retrieve a realistic, wise, and generous story about identity and difference as normal parts of our world. The story of Babel offers its readers a practical and useful view of difference that has been obscured by a long history of interpretation.[2]

The story of Babel is the Bible's story of the spread of humanity and the beginning of difference after the great flood. According to the larger biblical narrative in which it is located, a great flood destroyed everything, every living thing, except Noah and his family and two of every species of all the animals. A flood narrative such as this, in which a worldwide deluge ends the first era of world history and begins a second era, is actually common in other literature from the biblical world. We will return to the flood as the beginning of a new age in chapter 2. For now we need to know that the story of Babel appears right after the flood at the beginning of the second era of world history. It therefore describes how the new world began, and it explains how the world came to look like the world in which the Storyteller himself lived.

The story of Babel is a narrative in two parts. In the first part, human beings control the action and begin to reconstruct life again for themselves in the new era after the great flood (Gen 11:1-4). At the midpoint of the story, God comes down to find out what the human beings are doing (11:5). In the second part of the story, God controls the action. God responds to what human beings are doing and creates difference (Gen 11:6-9). As we reexamine the story, we will take its two-part structure seriously, and we will examine carefully each of its two parts.

---

2. More detailed and technical evidence for the interpretation of the story of Babel offered here is found in Theodore Hiebert, "The Tower of Babel and the Origin of the World's Cultures," *Journal of Biblical Literature* 126 no. 1 (2007): 29–58.

Creating a Common Culture: Genesis 11:1-4

¹All people* on earth had one language and the same words. ²When they traveled east, they found a valley in the land of Shinar and settled there. ³They said to each other, "Come, let's make bricks and bake them hard." They used bricks for stones and asphalt for mortar. ⁴They said, "Come, let's build for ourselves a city and a tower with its top in the sky, and let's make a name for ourselves so that we won't be dispersed over all the earth." (*Hebrew lacks *people*)

In this, the first half of the story, the Storyteller tells us how the first people in the new age of world history after the great flood set about re-creating life for themselves. When he begins their story of rebuilding society, the Storyteller starts with their common language: "All people on earth had one language and the same words." Their common language is the primary marker of a new and viable culture. It's the first thing the Storyteller tells us about the people of Babel (11:1). It's the first thing God notices when God comes down in the middle of the story (11:5) to see what the people have accomplished: "There is now one people and they all have one language" (11:6). And it's the first thing God responds to when God takes action to diversify human culture in the second half of the story: "Come, let's go down and mix up their language" (11:7).

After describing their common language, the Storyteller describes the people's efforts to put down roots in their own land. The people settle in Shinar, an area of the great Mesopotamian river valley, and today part of the modern country of Iraq. Together with the Nile Valley of Egypt, Mesopotamia was one of the two great ancient centers of civilization in ancient West Asia. The people begin by constructing a city with a tower out of fired mud brick (11:2-3), the typical building material in Mesopotamia. Their aim in building their city is simple: so "we won't be dispersed over all the earth." They wish to establish a particular homeland for themselves. And the way they do this is to begin building the institutions that characterize the ancient kingdoms the Storyteller knew: a chief city with fortified walls and towers that represented the center of a people's territory. This is as true for the great and dominant civilizations of Mesopotamia and Egypt as it is for the small, marginal countries in their orbits, such as the Storyteller's own kingdom of Judah with its primary city of Jerusalem.

A common language and a common land are two of the most fundamental markers of any group's cultural identity, from antiquity to the present. And our Storyteller shapes his narrative to highlight them. In the first words of the story, the Storyteller tells us the people speak a single language, and in the final words of the story's first half, he describes the people's efforts to claim a land and to put down roots. The world's first people have set about building the world's first culture at the beginning of history's new age.

After describing their common language and their common land, the Storyteller introduces one more important aspect of the people's project to build their culture: "let's make a name for ourselves" (11:4). In the biblical world, "name" signifies "identity," and making a name means establishing a unique identity with an esteemed reputation that will endure. It is an honorable and noble venture. We might think of the people's aim to make a name as the people's wish to articulate their distinctive identity, to define themselves, to answer for themselves the most basic question: "Who am I?" We might think of their aim to make a name as the people's wish to establish their sense of belonging, dignity, and pride in their culture.

A collective name, as sociologists point out, is one of the primary markers of a distinctive culture. It defines and articulates a common cultural identity. Biblical authors use "name" in this way for their own people Israel to describe their distinctiveness and status among the nations, as does the prophet Zephaniah, when he says, " 'I will provide you a name [identity] and a praiseworthy place among all the peoples of the earth,' says the LORD" (Zeph 3:20, author's translation). Israel's historians use "name" in this way for its great kings, in particular King David (2 Sam 7:9; 8:13), founder of their greatest dynasty in Jerusalem and Judah, during which our own Storyteller lived. The prophet Nathan delivers this divine message to David: "I will make your name [identity] as honorable as the most honorable men on earth" (2 Sam 7:9, author's translation). In the story of Babel, the Storyteller uses the phrase "make a name" to describe the first people in the world after the flood, seeking to establish—as all cultures following them would aim to do—their own unique, esteemed, and lasting identity in the world. The way a city and its enduring legacy create a lasting identity are both captured in this brief observation by Israel's sage, Ben Sira: "Children and building a city establish one's name" (*Ben Sira* 40:19).

The first half of the story of Babel, therefore, describes the first human effort to create a new common culture with a distinct identity. To do so, the Storyteller uses three of the most common markers of ethnicity: language, land, and name. He describes their project in an entirely realistic and positive way. The first thing the world's first people did after the flood is what all people have sought to do: create and preserve a distinct identity. The Storyteller observed this in the world in which he himself lived, in his own land of Judah and its primary city of Jerusalem with its Davidic dynasty, and in all the societies surrounding him on all sides.

Belonging to a distinctive cultural community with its own ethnic identity is, of course, a fundamental part of human experience, as important for the Storyteller then as it is for us today. It gives its members a unique identity, a sense of who they are in the world. It provides them with a sense of belonging to a community with shared values. It gives them a visible and recognized presence in the world, a pride in their culture, and the experience of affirmation and self-respect that an old and honorable cultural tradition provides. It encourages them to value, maintain, and pass on

9

their distinctive traditions to new generations. It is not surprising that re-creating society by creating a common cultural identity that would endure is the first task the people set for themselves in the new world.

Contemporary readers might be surprised that two of the most common markers of cultural identity today, skin color and religious affiliation, are not part of this story. Skin color, as we have seen in the introduction, is not a marker of ethnic identity in the Bible at all. Though it has become a prominent marker of difference in America and other countries today, our Storyteller, as with the other biblical authors of Genesis, does not use skin color to define difference.

Religion, by contrast, is a prominent marker of cultural identity in the Bible. In some biblical texts, such as the book of Deuteronomy, religion is considered the key marker of cultural identity and distinctiveness. So it may be somewhat surprising that religion does not play a role in defining cultural identity for the Storyteller who presents the story of Babel. In fact, our Storyteller never uses religion as a marker of cultural identity in his other stories in Genesis, as we will see in chapters 2 and 3. This is true also for the Priest, the other major writer of Genesis. We will talk more about the significance of this when we encounter these other stories about difference later in chapters 2 and 3.

Culture Becomes Suspect

In spite of the positive way that the Storyteller describes the first people's interest in discovering, establishing, and preserving a distinctive cultural identity for themselves, most readers through the centuries have found their project to reconstruct society after the flood to be sinful and malicious. Because these readings of the story have almost completely erased the story's original intent, we must take some time to acknowledge these readings and to explain how and why they came about. The oldest and most virulent misreading of the story views the human activity at the story's beginning as an act of pride and an attempt to assert human autonomy over against God. Readers came to this mistaken conclusion because of the story's tower.

Interpreters thought the tower was the key to unlock the meaning of the entire story, and they thought it implied rebellious pride. In fact, as James Kugel noted, it's only because readers have taken the tower as the key to the story's meaning that we now call this story "The *Tower* of Babel."[3] Readers took the tower to represent pride, not because of anything ominous the Storyteller says about it, but because it's what they thought it *implied*. They thought the phrase "a tower with its top in the sky," usually translated "a tower with its top in the heavens," meant that the people built it in order to *get into* heaven. The earliest interpreter of the story we have on record, the author of *Jubilees*, thought this, and he added this information to the story when he retold it. He wrote, "they built the city and the tower, *saying, 'Let us ascend on it into heaven.'* When we compare all the other uses of this common phrase, "with its top in the sky," in the Bible and in other literature of ancient West Asia outside of the Bible, we find it to be a simple cliché meaning "very tall," like the English term *skyscraper*. It never implies sinful pride or describes people building tall structures to scale heaven or to attack God. And our Storyteller does not say that it means that here.

Furthermore, the tower is not the Storyteller's center of attention. He is hardly interested in it at all. He mentions it only twice, and he includes it in the phrase "a city and a tower." Most likely, the Storyteller uses these two terms together to represent a single idea: an urban landscape including a tower. In this sense, the tower is one aspect of the cityscape the narrator describes rather than his primary interest. The Storyteller's marginal interest in the tower is reflected in the second half of the story, where the city

---

3. Kugel, *The Bible as It Was*, 123.

stands alone, and the tower disappears from the story entirely. He describes the end of the building project by saying, "they stopped building the city," without even mentioning the tower (11:8). Clearly, the detail that most intrigued readers, "the tower with its top in the sky," was of much less interest to the original Storyteller. And he says nothing ominous about it. We must remember that the only reason interpreters brought the tower to the center of the story was their mistake about what it *implied*.

In recent years, scholars have begun to recognize the secondary place of the tower in the story and the neutral meaning for the common cliché "its top in the sky." Some, still unable to give up the notion of pride, have shifted their attention from the tower to the people making a name for themselves as a possible clue to their malicious ambition. Such scholars think that making a name *implies* pride. These interpreters have even argued that it was because the people attempted to make a name *for themselves* that their attempt was proud and haughty, since in some places, such as the next episode of the Storyteller's narrative in Genesis 12:2, God makes Abraham's name great.[4] But as we have already seen, the phrase to "make a name" is an honorable act. It is the common goal of any culture to establish a unique identity with an esteemed reputation that will endure. And this is true in the Bible whether God makes someone's name great or whether individuals achieve this for themselves, as we see in the narratives of the hero David, founder of the great Davidic dynasty (2 Sam 7:9; 8:13). Biblical usage clearly shows us, as we have already seen, that making a name is not a self-centered act, a sinful expression of pride, or an attempt to establish human autonomy from God. It represents people's search for cultural identity, distinction, and respect.

Another feature of the story that some recent interpreters have taken to imply pride, is the city itself. These interpreters view city building as a symbol of human self-sufficiency, autonomy, and

---

4. E.g., Victor Hamilton, *The Book of Genesis 1–17* (Grand Rapids, MI: Eerdmans, 1990), 372.

hubris.[5] To read the story in this way means that we must import a negative view of cities from outside the story itself. A survey of our Storyteller's larger narrative of the origins of the world and of Israel in Genesis, to which this story belongs, reveals no anti-city polemic. In fact, it's unlikely that the Bible as a whole contains any true anti-urban ideology at all. The central and powerful role that the city of Jerusalem plays in the Davidic dynasty, in which our Storyteller lived, suggests that the Storyteller considered the city, as we have already seen, as one of the core anchors of cultural identity. Nothing in the story of Babel suggests otherwise.

These three popular ways of reading this story as a story of human pride are all misunderstandings of the story, in spite of the tight grip they have had on its interpretation and the deep and widespread influence they have exerted on the way the story has been understood. To understand the story properly, we must set aside these filters and read the story afresh, as we have just done. When we do so, we find a story about a people at the beginning of world history engaged in the first attempt in the new era to discover, create, and preserve their own cultural identity.

In the last few decades of biblical scholarship, a new but related misunderstanding of the story of Babel has become widely popular. This is the postcolonial reading of this story, which regards the Babel narrative as an anti-empire story. Reading the story this way also attributes pride to the builders of the city, but not the general human pride of rebellion against God and God's authority. In the postcolonial reading of this story, the human actors are not the first post-flood generation, acting alone in an archetypal way to re-create human culture. Rather, they are led by royal figures with imperial pretentions. These imperialists want to extend their power, expand their colonial reach, and impose their culture as dominant over the culture of others less powerful than they. The conclusion of the story names the city Babel

5. E.g., Frank S. Frick, *The City in Ancient Israel* (Missoula, MT: Scholars Press, 1977), 208.

(11:9), the biblical term for Babylon, which was the empire that harassed Judah and destroyed Jerusalem in the sixth century BCE. So, some of these more recent readers see the story as a critique of the Babylonian Empire in particular. The people's attempt to create and preserve a single culture is reinterpreted as the imposition of a single dominant culture on other cultures by a royal imperial power. And the story is understood to be a critique of the violent suppression of difference by colonial powers intent on establishing one dominant culture.[6]

In fact, some of the very earliest readers of this story already read it in this more specific way as an anti-empire story directed against the Babylonian Empire. In the first century CE, Jewish historian Flavius Josephus imported the figure of Nimrod from Genesis 10:8-10, where Nimrod is associated with the city of Babel, into his interpretation of this story. According to Josephus, Nimrod spearheaded the building project in the Babel story and "incited the people to insolence and contempt toward God."[7] God's response in the second half of the story is therefore an attack on Babylon and its pretensions. This reading, since Babylon is such a powerful imperial antagonist in the Bible, has been revived as an element of postcolonial readings of the Babel story today.

In our era, voices from the margins have risen in biblical scholarship to retrieve and emphasize the Bible's stand against colonialism, against the oppressive policies and practices of dominant cultures of antiquity that imposed their cultural norms on others, that dehumanized neighboring peoples, and that destroyed those offering any resistance, as did Judah and Jerusalem under Babylonian rule. This is a powerful and persistent theme in biblical texts, in particular in the words of the prophets, who spoke fearlessly against the arrogance of cultural domination. Contemporary scholars have drawn more and more attention to this aspect of

6. E.g., J. Severino Croatto, "A Reading of the Story of the Tower of Babel from a Perspective of Non-Idenity," in *Teaching the Bible: The Discourses and Politics of Biblical Pedagogy,* ed. Fernando F. Segovia and Mary Ann Tolbert (Maryknoll, NY: Orbis, 1998), 203–23.

7. Jospehus, *Antiquities* 1.113–14.

biblical thought in our postcolonial era. Their work has provided a growing, indispensable, and overdue critique of the abuses of dominant cultures and the way in which the Bible speaks against this abuse of power, but also the ways the Bible has been enlisted to support those in power and their suppression of difference.

Yet, as we have seen, the project in the first half of our story, though it describes a city named Babel, is not about empire, its hubris, its colonial ambitions, or its imposition of a dominant culture. It's about the discovery, creation, and construction of cultural identity at the beginning of history after the great flood. The story about building Babel in Genesis 11:1-4 mentions no king or empire with imperial pretentions. Rather, it attributes the entire project to the people as a whole, using plural pronouns and verbs throughout. No uniquely royal or imperial language is present. Furthermore, the idea of empire does not fit the aim of this narrative in its larger context. This story is about the entire human race before the differentiation of cultures, not about one culture imposing its will on another. The single language everyone speaks is not imposed by imperial edict but is the natural reality of a single family surviving the flood. The aim of the project is not to extend an empire through colonial expansion but to establish and maintain a common culture in one place. This story of Babel is therefore not about the suppression of difference by one dominant culture. It is about the reconstruction of culture itself and, in the second half of the story, to which we now turn, about its diversification into many cultures.

It is not surprising that the old interpretation of the story of Babel as an imperial project led by the monarch Nimrod would be revived in new dress in the postcolonial era. While postcolonial aims to expose the ways in which power suppressed difference in many biblical settings are crucial, I believe the beginning of the story of Babel is dealing with another equally important human experience—the need for meaning, belonging, and identity that can only come from being a member of a common cultural tradition. By beginning his narrative of the new world with the human aim to create an identity in a common culture, our Storyteller embraces our basic human need for belonging, dignity, and identity that such a culture provides. He describes a fundamental need for social identity that all share.

Creating Cultural Diversity: Genesis 11:5-9

⁵Then the LORD came down to see the city and the tower that the humans built. ⁶And the LORD said, "There is now one people and they all have one language. This is what they have begun to do, and now all that they plan to do will be possible for them. ⁷Come, let's go down and mix up [multiply] their language[s] there so they won't understand each other's language." ⁸Then the LORD dispersed them from there over all the earth, and they stopped building the city. ⁹Therefore, it is named Babel, because there the LORD mixed up [multiplied] the language of all the earth; and from there the LORD dispersed them over all the earth.

In the first half of the story of Babel, the people who began life on earth again after the flood engage in the most basic of all human endeavors. They attempt to create a common cultural identity, to which they would belong and that they could pass on to future generations. The Storyteller views belonging to a distinct culture with its own identity as normal, as a part of the reality of the world in which he lived. He sees constructing a common culture as an expected, natural, and respectable thing for the world's first people to do. In the second half of the story, God enters the narrative to diversify culture. Just as the world's people are constructing a single culture, God introduces many cultures. God introduces difference. How we understand what God intended and what God did when God brought difference into the world will have everything to do with how we understand the message of this story about difference and the Storyteller's own attitude toward it. And to understand what God intended and what God did, we must reexamine the details of God's words and actions carefully, because Genesis's readers have understood them in destructive and troubling ways.

At the midpoint of the story, God appears on earth to see what the new world's first people are doing (11:5). First, God describes what God sees: "There is now one people and they all have one language" (11:6a). God sees first what the Storyteller told us first about the world's people: "All people on earth had one language and the same words" (11:1). God notices precisely what the Storyteller recognized as the primary marker of a distinct culture: a common language.

God calls these first post-flood humans speaking a common language are "one people." The word "people," or *am* in biblical Hebrew, can be used in the very general way we use it, but it also has a much more precise meaning than this English translation does. The Hebrew word *am* is primarily a kinship term used for a particular group that traces itself back to a common ancestor to whom all its members are related. So biblical Israel, for example, is commonly referred to as "*am* Israel," that is, all those tracing themselves back to their ancestor Israel/Jacob. By using the term "one people," God identifies the first humans God sees not as a diffuse group of individuals but as a kinship society with a common ancestry and a single, shared culture.

Thus, God sees just what the Storyteller describes in the story's first part. God sees the world's first people engaged in creating a distinctive common culture. When God begins a response with the words "There is now..." God locates this event right at the beginning of the world's new age. We might paraphrase God's description of what God sees as something like this: "Right now, the entire world has one ethnic group tracing itself to a single ancestor and speaking the same language." Or, "The world is beginning again with a single distinctive culture."

In God's second sentence, God comes to a conclusion about what God sees: "This is what they have begun to do, and now all that they plan to do will be possible for them" (11:6b). We must examine this sentence with special care, since it has been the place in the story where readers have found negative attitudes both toward the people's construction of identity at the beginning of the story and toward God's diversification of culture in this part of the story. And these negative attitudes have been perpetuated in many English translations. So, some careful grammatical work is necessary.

Let's begin with the Hebrew verbs in the first phrase, "this is what they have begun to do." The verbs are infinitives, that is, they contain no tense, so the translator must supply it. A literal and wooden translation of the Hebrew might be something like, "this is their beginning to do." In the context of the story, either the present perfect tense, "this is what they have begun to do," or the present tense, "this is what they are beginning to do," is the simplest and most sensible choice. To paraphrase just a bit, using the present tense, we could translate, "This is what they're starting to do." That is, God recognizes just what the Storyteller has already described in the first half of the story: the people are in the beginning stages of constructing a single culture.

Then God comes to this conclusion: "now all that they plan to do will be possible for them" (11:6). A very literal and wooden translation of the actual Hebrew syntax might be something like this: "now not will be withheld from them all that they plan to do." God concludes that the people will be successful. God realizes that the people will accomplish the task they've set out for themselves, in which they are now in the beginning stages, to create a single distinctive culture. We could thus paraphrase God's entire observation in 11:6 in this way: "It looks like this single ethnic group speaking a common language will be able to carry out what they've started, that is, create a single common culture for themselves." In God's speech, God describes what God sees and recognizes the people's eventual success.

Then God acts. After seeing this human activity (11:5), recognizing the cultural uniformity of the first humans (11:6a), and acknowledging the probable success of their plan to preserve it (11:6b), God intervenes to introduce the world's different cultures. To achieve this, God takes two actions: God multiplies the languages of the world's first people (11:7), and then God disperses them to different geographical locations across the earth (11:8). In order to describe God's acts to diversify human culture in this way, the Storyteller focuses on the two primary markers of culture with which the Storyteller began his story: a common language and a common living space.

Language, as we have already seen, was regarded by our Storyteller, as it is by anthropologists and sociologists today, as one of the primary markers of distinct cultures or ethnic groups. Just as the Storyteller used a common language as the first marker of the people's common culture in the first half of the story, so he uses multiple languages as the first marker of multiple cultures when God diversifies cultures in the second half of the story. Our Storyteller's view that language is a primary marker of cultural distinctiveness and difference is shared by many other biblical writers. In the Bible's other account of the spread of humanity across the world after the flood in Genesis 10, which we will look at in more detail in a moment, the Priest also differentiates peoples from one another by the different languages they speak (Gen 10:5, 20, 31). Israel's historians (Deut 28:49), prophets (Isa 66:18; Zech 8:23), and psalmists (Ps 81:5) also view different languages as key markers of cultural difference.

Our Storyteller uses the Hebrew verb *balal*, "mix," when God acts to introduce different languages on earth: "Come, let's go down and mix their language" (11:7); "there the Lord mixed the language of all the earth" (11:9). Elsewhere in the Bible, *balal* is used for mixing fine flour and oil to make offertory cakes or bread (e.g., Exod 29:40; Lev 14:10). We should understand this verb here to mean that God prepares a mixture of languages, a polyglot world, so that the language of humanity is no longer a single language but a mixture of many languages. As we will see in a moment, translators have commonly used harshly negative translations, in particular "confuse" and "confound," for *balal* in this story, even though biblical evidence provides no support for these translations. The verb simply means "mix."

The Storyteller chose this rare Hebrew word to describe God's multiplying or diversifying the world's languages—God's creating a mixture of global languages—because he wanted to explain the origin of the name Babel, the city from which all the peoples with their different languages spread out. "Therefore, it is named Babel [*bavel*], because there the LORD mixed [*balal*] the language of all the earth" (11:9). According to the rules of modern linguistics, these two words are not actually related to one another linguistically, since they do not derive from the same root term. But our Storyteller often finds connections through words that sound very much like one another (a quasi-homophone). And that is what he has done here.

God's second act when God intervenes to introduce the world's diverse cultures is to give the world's first post-flood people different lands to inhabit. "Then the LORD dispersed them from there over all the earth" (11:8, cf. 11:9 CEB). Just as the Storyteller described the people's wish to establish a common homeland as a key marker of their common culture in the first half of the story, so he describes God's dispersal of the people to different geographical regions across the world as a key marker of the world's new cultural diversity in the second half of the story. By saying that the people "stopped building the city" (11:8), the Storyteller tells us that the people's aim to secure a single common territory centered on their city has ended, and the new era of multiple cultures inhabiting different lands has begun. In the Bible's other account of the spread of humanity across the world after the flood in Genesis 10, the Priest too differentiates peoples from one another by the different lands they occupy (Gen 10:5, 20, 31).

This Storyteller shares with other biblical authors the view that Babel and its environs, the "valley in the land of Shinar"

(11:2)—biblical terms for ancient Babylon and Mesopotamia—was the cradle of ancient civilization, and the area, in fact, from which his own ancestors migrated. He claims that his own lineage, the family of Terah, from whom Abraham, Isaac, and Jacob descend, originated in Mesopotamia, "their native land," and then migrated westward to Canaan (Gen 11:28-30; 15:7; 24:7). The Priest too places Israel's origins in Mesopotamia (Gen 11:31), as does the historian who describes Israel's entry into Canaan (Josh 24:2-3). In fact, the name *Hebrew* itself came to be understood as "one from beyond," signifying Israel's origins in Mesopotamia, the region beyond the river Euphrates. So the Storyteller's people too, in a very particular way, spread out from their origin in Mesopotamia.

Our Storyteller thus employs two key cultural markers, language and land, to describe the world's first single culture, on the one hand (11:1-4), and the world's different cultures, on the other hand (11:7-9). The close relationship between separate locations and separate languages is an important concept in historical linguistics, in which the development of new languages is directly linked to a space-time continuum. Over time, communities living in different geographical regions develop different languages. Our Storyteller is not a modern linguist, as his explanation of the name Babel shows, but his story does reflect an ancient observation about different cultures, about the connection between the different regions they inhabit and the different languages they speak. Taken together, God's two actions, distinguishing languages and dispersing humanity, explain the beginning of difference and the origin of the world's cultures.

Identity and Difference as Normal

Having reexamined the story's details carefully, we are now in a position to ask about the story's attitude toward difference, about its view of the world's cultural diversity. Answering these questions is a challenge, because the story is so short and so action oriented. It tells us what the people did, and then it tells us what God did. But it doesn't tell us why they did what they did. It doesn't enter the minds of the characters to tell us what the people's motives were or what God's motives were. It doesn't tell us what they were thinking, and that's what we're most interested in. So, we determine the story's attitude toward difference from the events and flow of the story itself.

As we have already seen, the story describes the post-flood world's first people's efforts to establish a shared culture in a straightforward and positive way. While speaking a common language, they set about building a city and creating an identity ("making a name") in order to put down roots in a specific territory. They aim to build the kind of common culture to which the Storyteller himself belongs and that he observes among his neighbors in the world around him. The story presents the people's desire to establish and preserve a common culture without blame or disapproval. The Storyteller does not claim the people disobeyed God, sinned, or acted evilly, in direct contrast to his earlier stories of Eden's garden, Cain and Abel, and the great flood. Nor does he imply by anything the people did that they were proud, defiant, or rebellious. In stark contrast to traditional and cynical readings of the story, the Storyteller describes the people pursuing one of the most elemental human needs: building a culture in which they could find identity and belonging.

As we have now seen in our reexamination of the second half of the story, it describes God's acts introducing multiple cultures in a similarly straightforward and positive way. When God speaks, God recognizes two facts: that the people are constructing a single unified culture, and that they will be successful in achieving their goal. When God acts, God introduces multiple cultures by multiplying the people's lands and languages. Nothing in God's words or deeds suggests that God punishes, judges, or curses the people.

Nor do God's words or deeds imply that God has unleashed a catastrophe on the world, producing chaos and confusion, though interpreters for generations have read the story in this way, as we will see in a moment. On the contrary, God sees the people establishing a single culture, and then God introduces many cultures.

This dramatic tension at the heart of the story, in which the people construct a single culture and God introduces multiple cultures, raises core questions: Does God thereby disapprove of the people's work? Was there something wrong with the people's efforts? And did God introduce difference and diversify culture as a negative response to the people's deeds, as a punishment of any kind? The story does not allow us to answer yes to any of these questions or to problematize either the people's activity or God's response. The story never criticizes the people's efforts, nor does it describe God's response in negative terms. It does not present the people's work and God's work as oppositional efforts or incompatible goals. By diversifying cultures, God doesn't eliminate the distinctive cultures people build; God simply multiplies them. God doesn't erase the human effort to create common cultures that provide identity and belonging; God simply introduces many of these distinct cultures. The people's work and God's work are not contradictory. They are complementary.

This story is wrestling with the profound tension at the heart of human experience between identity and difference, between the power of cultural solidarity on the one hand, and the reality of cultural diversity on the other. In its first half, the story acknowledges and describes the reality of cultural solidarity arising from the deep human need for identity, for belonging to a society whose members share a common language, living space, and identity. In its second half, the story acknowledges and accounts for the reality of cultural difference. In spite of the human desire and need for identity and cultural solidarity, the world is actually made up of extraordinary cultural diversity. In articulating this tension, the Storyteller represents the drive toward identity and solidarity as a distinctively human impulse, and the emergence of difference as a distinctively divine choice.

Attributing difference, the extravagant array of the world's cultures, to God's actions represents a belief on the part of our Storyteller that God as the creator brought everything God knew into existence, including the world's profusion of cultures. But the drama of the story suggests something more. The Storyteller also recognizes the depth of the human need for identity and cultural solidarity, so that, left to themselves, humans—in this case, the world's first people after the flood—would dedicate their efforts to preserving a common culture. How in a world in which membership in a kinship group with a common culture defined human life in all respects, and outside of which a person had no standing, could difference possibly emerge? In such a world, our Storyteller considered cultural difference possible only as part of a larger divine design, a design implemented by God's own initiative. Difference is God's idea.

Difference Becomes Dangerous

It is striking that a story that embraces both cultural solidarity and cultural difference as normal in this open way would have been read for so long as such a negative tale, in which cultural solidarity is linked to rebellious pride and cultural diversity to divine punishment. But this is exactly the way this story's interpreters have read it through the years. We have already seen how the story's interpreters turned the first half of the story into an account of human rebellion against God. Now we must look briefly at how they turned the second half of the story into an account of God's punishment on humanity.

This story's readers have turned God's creation of a diverse world into a punishment on its people by two crucial moves. First, they invested God's speech with ominous threats and fears.

Reading God's speech in this way has been so important for understanding diversity as punishment that we need to explain this misreading of God's words and their harmful effects in detail. When God speaks, as we have already seen, God recognizes the people's single culture and God concludes that the people will be able to preserve it: "And the LORD said, 'There is now one people and they all have one language. This is what they have begun to do, and now all that they plan to do will be possible for them" (11:6 CEB).

Most English translations today translate this verse ominously. And they do this not because the Hebrew requires it but because they themselves have inherited the traditional "pride and punishment" interpretation of the story. In this half of the story, translators turn a simple and direct description of God's creation of the world's diverse cultures into an impending catastrophe. They do this in several steps. First, many translate the opening Hebrew term *hen*, "now," with the less-common translation "if," a meaning that our Storyteller never uses for the term. This turns the opening main clause of God's speech, "There is now one people and they all have one language," into a subordinate clause, suggesting that the people's common culture will lead to the impending dangers implied by the next phrases of God's speech: "*If* as one people speaking the same language..." (NIV, cf. NAB, NJPS).

Second, some translators use the future tense rather than the present or past tense for the infinitive verbs in God's next phrase, so that God's simple observation, "This is what they have begun to do" (CEB) becomes an ominous fear: "This is only the beginning of what they will do" (NRSV, cf. RSV, JB). With a future-tense translation, translators shift God's attention from what God actually sees when God inspects the human project to an event God fears might happen, which is completely outside the bounds of the story itself. While a future meaning for the tense-less infinitive verbs is grammatically possible, it is clearly not the most obvious meaning of this phrase in the context of the story itself, where God simply describes what God sees. The translators of the NRSV exaggerate this future fear even more by adding the word "only," not found in the Hebrew, to their translation: "This is *only* the beginning of what they will do." Nothing in the story, except the traditional interpretation that the people were about to storm heaven, would suggest that God reacted with fear about the future.

In a third step, translators have exaggerated and added foreboding to God's assessment of human intentions in their translation of God's last comment. As with God's previous comment, a simple observation, "now all that they plan to do will be possible for them" (CEB), is turned into an ominous fear, "nothing that they propose to do will now be impossible for them" (NRSV, cf. NIV, NAB). God's conclusion that the people will succeed in building and preserving a common culture becomes God's judgment that the people are entirely out of control and will attempt anything to challenge God. Again, nothing in what God sees the people doing would warrant such a response. Only the interpretation of the first part of the story as an attack on God would provoke such a reaction. And, as we have already seen, the people attempted no such thing.

After God's speech, God acts to introduce cultural diversity— not to punish pride, nor to beat back a future challenge to God's authority, nor to restrain human arrogance, nor to curse people for their sins. But another fateful translation has reinforced that impression. That is the punitive translation of the Hebrew term *balal*, "mix," as "confuse" or "confound": "Come, let us go down and confuse their language" (11:7 NIV). No other translation in the story has done more than this one to say that difference is dangerous. The unwarranted negative understanding of *balal* goes back to the Greek translation of the Hebrew scriptures in the third century BCE. Major modern translations like the NIV and NRSV perpetuate it. And recent individual translators trying to capture the Hebrew wordplay of *balal/bavel* emphasize it with translations like "babble their language" or "baffle their language."[8] As much as any single translation in the entire story, translating *balal* as "confuse" has equated God's diversification of culture with chaos, confusion, and conflict in the minds of the story's readers. It has defined difference as disorder and strife. As we have seen, *balal* means "mix" or "prepare a mixture," and there is no evidence, except negative interpretive lenses, for giving it such a bleak translation.

One last detail in the story has implied to many of its readers that God's act to diversify culture is an act of divine judgment. That detail is the city's name, Babel. As we have already seen, the Mesopotamian river valley, in which Babel was located, was considered by our Storyteller as one of the birthplaces of civilization and the origin of Israel's own ancestors. But later in biblical history, Babel, the biblical name for the ancient city of Babylon, became a powerful empire, eventually colonizing the entire coast of the Mediterranean Sea, destroying the city of Jerusalem, and bringing Judah under its control. Subsequently in biblical texts, Babylon became the core symbol of the evil empire. From this time on, it was almost impossible not to read this older story as a story about the evil empire, its violence against Israel and Judah, and its judgment by God. God's diversification of humanity was thus swept up into this act of punishment.

Genesis Maps the World's Diversity

We can no longer read Genesis 11:1-9 as this kind of a narrative of pride and punishment and as the climax of sin and judgment at the beginning of Genesis, as we have done for so long. We now understand its role in the book of Genesis in an entirely new way. We read the story of Babel as God's introduction of

---

8. Richard Elliot Friedman, *Commentary on the Torah* (San Francisco: HarperSanFrancisco, 2001), 46; David Rosenberg, in Harold Bloom's *The Book of J* (New York: Grove Weidenfeld, 1990), 73.

difference into the world at the very beginning of the new age after the flood. As such, this story does not stand alone in Genesis. It is actually the starting point for the entire book of Genesis that follows. From this story onward, both the Storyteller and the Priest, through their genealogies and genealogical narratives, map out the diversity of the entire world in which they live. Their central interest from Babel on is to describe the diverse cultures of the post-flood world created there, to explain these cultures' relationships to one another, and to situate their own culture and their own identity within the diverse world that God brought into existence.

Our Storyteller actually states his interest in the new world's diversity even before his Babel story, at the end of his account of the flood, when he writes, "The sons of Noah who left the ark were Shem, Ham, and Japheth, Ham being the father of Canaan. These three were Noah's sons, and from these all people of the earth were dispersed" (Gen 9:18-19, author's translation). His story of Babel, then, explains how this dispersion came about. When he concludes the story of Babel with this sentence, "And from there the LORD dispersed them over all the earth," the Storyteller echoes his last sentence in the flood narrative. In the remainder of Genesis, the Storyteller documents the origins of new cultures in the post-flood world. He preserves in his traditions some genealogical information describing the branching out of humanity among Shem's descendants, to whom he traces his own lineage (Gen 10:21, 24-30; 11:28-30), and also among Ham's descendants (10:8-19). But he is especially interested in the lineages that branch off later from Abraham and who become Israel's closest neighbors: the Ishmaelites (16:1-14), the Moabites and Ammonites (19:30-38), and the Edomites (25:21-34; 33:15-18).

Within his map of the world and the origins of its different cultures in Genesis, the Storyteller explains his own origins and identity as a member of the Israelite people. In order to do that, he focuses in a particular way on the lineage from which the

Israelites emerge, from Noah, to Shem, to Eber and his sons, to Terah, Abraham, Isaac, and to Jacob, also known as Israel. In the Storyteller's genealogies and genealogical narratives, he aims to give an account of his own place and his own identity among the different cultures of his world. While focusing on his own lineage, he is always intent on recognizing his culture as one among many different ones, and he is always interested in the origins of these other cultures and in explaining Israel's relationship to them. Our Storyteller is, therefore, interested in what it means to be a part of a diverse world and to live with difference. We will say more about this in chapters 2 and 3.

Our Storyteller's interest in the beginning of difference in the post-flood world is shared by the other author of the world's early history in Genesis, the Priest. In the Priest's account of God's covenant with Noah and the entire earth after the flood, God's first words introduce this theme: "Be fertile, multiply, and fill the earth" (Gen 9:1, cf. 9:7). The Priest's account of the outcome of God's command to fill the earth is found in his great genealogical record in Genesis 10, which scholars describe as a Table of Nations. It's the Priest's "parallel" to the Storyteller's story of Babel in Genesis 11. It records the Priest's traditions about the manner in which humanity multiplies, diversifies, and fills the earth after the flood, from a single monocultural family to the diverse world in which he lives. The Priest divides his Table of Nations into three sections, one for each of Noah's sons: Japheth (10:2-5), Ham (10:6-20), and Shem (10:21-31). Each section ends with a summary statement describing the diversification of the descendants of that son, such as this one describing Shem's descendants: "These are Shem's descendants, according to their kinship groups, languages, lands, and nations" (10:31, author's translation; cf. 10:5, 20). Just like the Storyteller, the Priest distinguishes distinctive cultures by the markers of language, land, and descent. The Priest concludes his entire genealogy with this summary of the beginnings of difference in the post-flood world: "From these the nations in the earth spread out after the flood" (10:32, author's translation).

Thus, both great recorders of beginnings in the book of Genesis are intensely interested in the beginning of difference in the new world—their world—in the post-flood age. And they both regard the origins of cultural difference as God's idea and as God's intention for their world. They respect the human drive toward identity and toward a distinct culture. And they recognize the validity of the distinctive cultures around them, including their own Israelite culture, that emerged out of this drive. At the same time, they take the multiplicity of the world's distinctive cultures as the reality of the world. Even more, they describe cultural difference as God's design for the world.

Reading Babel Today

The three-thousand-year-old story of Babel remains strikingly contemporary and real. It probes the most basic issues about identity and difference that societies have faced through history and continue to face today. Most in today's world feel that deep tensions surrounding difference are sharper than ever in the current climate of cultural relationships and political rhetoric. In the United States, it is clear that we do not live in a post-racial society, that we are not able to find a constructive response to immigration, and that political processes are increasingly polarized. Many have experienced exclusion based on difference in new and more destructive ways. Nationalist and isolationist movements and leaders across the globe have created new tensions between nations.

Read in its traditional way, the story of Babel reinforces these present-day tensions about difference. The traditional reading teaches that difference is dangerous. It regards difference as God's punishment and as the source of confusion, conflict, and chaos.

Believing difference is dangerous leads to the suspicion, fear, and distancing of those who are different. It feeds into false stereotypes. It legitimates all the ways in which dominant cultures use their power to demonize, exclude, enslave, and eliminate those who are different from them. It reinforces nationalism and isolationism. This is a deadly place to begin thinking about difference and living with it.

Why our ancestors turned the story of Babel into a story of danger and why we have perpetuated this reading are deeply disturbing questions. They point to the very real tension in human experience between difference as dangerous and difference as instructive and enriching. We might blame the writer of *Jubilees*, the first interpreter of difference as dangerous in the story of Babel, for the tenacious negative trajectory of interpretation he set for his heirs. He was, in fact, an individual who saw the world through a sharp "us versus them" lens, who considered other nations impure and destined for destruction, and who thought his own people should separate themselves as much as possible from them. But we must also recognize the generations of readers, down to ourselves, who have embraced this reading of the story and its problematic view of difference. We must recognize our own hand in perpetuating this reading, and we must examine our own deep tendency to identify with this attitude toward difference as a punishment and a problem.

Rereading the story of Babel can open our eyes to the authentic ancient story. It can also open our eyes to our comfortable acceptance of the negative understanding of difference embedded in its traditional interpretation. It can open our eyes to our own unexamined attitudes toward difference that lie behind our acceptance of this traditional reading. Rereading Genesis 11 as a story that acknowledges and embraces both cultural solidarity and cultural difference gives us a new—really, very old—and positive starting point for thinking about difference. Not only does it give us an opportunity to reexamine the negative attitudes toward difference that have governed our traditional reading of this story, but it also provides a starting point for developing new and constructive views for thinking about and living with difference.

The story can be constructive for us in two key ways. First, the story of Babel embraces cultural solidarity. It recognizes the reality and the importance of ethnic identity. It knows how crucial it is for our lives as social beings to be part of a unique and distinctive culture. That was precisely the aim of the first humans following the flood, who wished to reestablish human community in their new world. This crucial human need to belong to a distinctive community, reflected in the people's work in the first half of the story of Babel, is captured in contemporary language by America Ferrera, who invited a diverse array of Americans to describe their own searches for identity, which she published in *American Like Me: Reflections on Life Between Cultures*.

> I grew up believing I was alone in feeling stuck between cultures. . . . I tried shaping an identity that would make sense to other people by shedding pieces of myself and attempting to assimilate. Ironically, the opportunities to fulfill my dreams were the ones that required me to embrace my unique identity. . . . I believe that culture shapes identity and defines possibility; that it teaches us who we are, what to believe, and how to dream.[9]

The crucial need for identity and belonging is also reflected in contemporary experience by Orlando Crespo in his book *Being Latino in Christ: Finding Wholeness in Your Ethnic Identity*.

> As human beings it is impossible to live outside of these integrated systems of beliefs, values, customs, and institutions, for they give us the connectedness and belonging that are essential to the human heart. It is in this environment of culture that God gives us the sense of identity and dignity that are necessary for physical, emotional, and mental wholeness.[10]

---

9. America Ferrera, ed., with E. Cayce Dumont, *American Like Me: Reflections on Life Between Cultures* (New York: Gallery Books, 2018), 303, xxii.

10. Orlando Crespo, *Being Latino in Christ: Finding Wholeness in Your Ethnic Identity* (Downers Grove, IL: IVP Books, 2003), 86.

At the same time, without qualification, the story of Babel also embraces difference. It does so by communicating two important things. The first is that difference is God's reality, the result of God's own activity in re-creating the world after the flood. The Storyteller believes the myriad different cultures surrounding him in the world in which he lives to be God's decision and God's intention. Just as he attributed the world of nature in which he lived to the creative activity of God at the beginning of time, as told in his creation narrative (Gen 2–3), so he attributed the world of cultural diversity to the creative activity of God after the flood. Difference is the reality of the world God made. Expressed in contemporary and less religious language, this view of difference is captured in Chimamanda Adichie's words quoted at the beginning of this chapter.

> Teach her about difference. Make difference ordinary. Make difference normal. Because difference is the reality of our world. And by teaching her about difference, you are equipping her to survive in a diverse world.[11]

The story of Babel teaches that difference is God's reality, and it also teaches that each distinctive culture has equal worth. This is the only conclusion we can draw from God's act to spread peoples across the world, each with its own language and its own geography. At the end of the story, there is no dominant, exceptional, or normative culture that is in a position of power or privilege to dominate, demean, marginalize, or eliminate other cultures. The world's field of cultures is a level one. The world is filled not with a single distinctive culture but with an array of distinctive cultures. True, the world's diversity originated at Babel, in one of the ancient cradles of civilization, but even work on that city ends when, at the conclusion of the story, that project is replaced with the reality of the world's diversity. Our Storyteller will continue his

---

11. Adichie, *Dear Ijeawele*, 61.

narrative with a special interest in his own culture, but he doesn't privilege that culture in the story of Babel when difference began.

Such a story about difference provides a powerful starting point for rethinking the value of difference and for countering the tensions, prejudices, and conflicts that difference can provoke. It teaches that difference is the way that God wanted the world to be. It teaches that difference is normal. It teaches that difference is the reality in which God intended the world's people to live. It teaches that all cultures were created equal. This way of thinking counters the "us versus them" way of thinking about difference. It counters the fear of difference present in so much contemporary political and nationalistic rhetoric. It counters stereotyping others as deficient and dangerous. It counters any attempt to legitimate a dominant culture with the power to dominate and colonize others. It provides a starting point for constructing a way of thinking of difference and living with it that begins with the idea that difference is real and proper and good.

By setting the people's quest for a distinctive cultural identity in relationship to God's act of introducing multiple cultures, our Storyteller has recognized the reality and essential role of both in the world in which he lived. The relationship between a strong cultural identity and the reality of cultural difference is not viewed by the Storyteller as antagonistic or contradictory. He sees them as complementary. He sees them as equally real and essential parts of human life. He may even have recognized the inherent connection between identity and difference, a connection expressed in contemporary language by Crespo.

> Many Americans fear emphasizing their cultural identity because this might lead to tribalism....A healthy ethnic identity should actually lead to *greater* appreciation for the differences of others, because you know how valuable your own distinctiveness is. Only in an environment where people are encouraged to pursue a healthy ethnic identity is diversity possible, since diversity is about equally affirming all the cultures and ethnicit[ies] that are present.[12]

---

12. Crespo, *Being Latino in Christ*, 85.

Identity and difference: The Storyteller places them side by side in his ancient story to say that both are real and normal. Both define human experience. And both are part of the world God made. This is a revolutionary way of reading the story of Babel. And it can be a revolutionary way of thinking about difference and living with it today.

Noah's Descendants: Biblical Writers Choose Their Family

I was born into a community of radical love. It echoed through my home and the streets of my neighborhood. Sunset Park was a noisy, happy place, filled with Palestinian, Dominican, Mexican, Ecuadoran, and Honduran families. A place where families and neighbors were one in the same. You did for your neighbor just as you would do for an immediate family member. . . . If I hadn't grown up believing that my neighbors are my family, I may not have cared, but it was in my nature to care about all these groups of people.

—Linda Sarsour, co-chair of the 2017 Women's March and former executive director of the Arab-American Association of New York.[1]

In chapter 1, we discovered the Bible's embrace of both ethnic identity and cultural difference expressed in the story of the Tower of Babel. We discovered that the Storyteller knows how essential ethnic identity is, since after the flood he describes the world's first people investing all their energy in creating a distinctive ethnic identity for themselves (Gen 11:1-4). We discovered also that the Storyteller recognizes the many different ethnicities around him as the normal reality for the world, since

---

1. Linda Sarsour, "Linda Sarsour," in *American Like Me: Reflections on Life Between Cultures*, ed. America Ferrera with E. Cayce Dumont (New York: Gallery Books, 2018), 283, 292.

he describes God creating them. He attributes the world's cultural diversity to God's own intention and intervention (Gen 11:5-9). He describes the diversity of his world as God's work, as the world God wanted.

In this chapter, we take a new look at what comes next. How do the Storyteller and the Priest view the *relationship* between identity and difference? How do they see themselves and their own particular ethnic identity in relation to the other ethnic identities in the world around them? How do they position themselves and the Israelite culture to which they belong among all the other distinctive cultures in the diverse world God brought about at Babel? How do they honor their own heritage and at the same time engage others different from theirs? What do they do about difference? Chapter 1 focused on the reality and normativity of ethnic identity and ethnic differences in the world. Now we will look at what comes after Babel to discover how biblical writers, as Israelites, describe their sense of their own identity and their encounter with difference in the world in which they live.

The Storyteller and the Priest constructed the entire book of Genesis to engage this very task, that is, to explain their identity in a diverse world. And to understand how they did this we will examine two crucial topics. The first is this: both these authors understood their own identity and their relationship to others in terms of family relationships, and they used their own family experience, structures, and language to explain this relationship. They thought in familial concepts and language because they were members of a kinship society in which family was everything. It determined the way they thought of themselves and of all their relationships. Their family structure defined the individual's identity and role in his or her immediate family. Their family structure determined each family's identity and its role in relation to other families in the village. As villages made up larger kinship groups, these groups made up tribes, and these tribes made up peoples, such as the people of Israel, all relationships were described in familial terms. Even relationships between peoples and other nations were conceived in familial terms. Ultimately, the people's relationship to God was understood as just such a familial relationship. One of the primary titles for God in ancient Israel is "father."

When the Storyteller and Priest set out to explain their identity in a diverse world, they thus use the mental framework and language of a family. In fact, they set up the book of Genesis as one gigantic family tree, a family tree that encompasses all the world's lineages, including the writers' own lineage of biblical Israel. This is the reason for all the genealogies that modern readers find so boring and difficult. In intricate and careful detail, these genealogies and the genealogical narratives that accompany them document every branch of the world's lineages and peoples, how they are related to one another, and ways in which Israel itself is related to each of them. The language of family and kinship will thus determine and define everything we have to say in the next two chapters about Israel's view of its own identity and of its relationship to others.

This perspective is not really controversial. That biblical Israel was a kinship society, and that it thought of all relationships in its world through this lens, is widely recognized and acknowledged. But few of us realize how crucial this is in understanding the shape and meaning of the book of Genesis. Few of us recognize how Genesis's authors put together their stories in the book of Genesis to construct Israel's great family tree. Few of us realize how deeply the dynamics of family relationships govern the understanding of biblical authors about their own identity and their relation to others. Yet this familial way of thinking about others exists in most traditional cultures around the globe, and it still exists among some in the United States today, as the words of Linda Sarsour illustrate. She thought of her neighborhood as "a place where families and neighbors were one and the same. You did for your neighbor just as you would do for an immediate family member."[2] Identity and difference as family matters will be one of the most fundamental themes in the pages that follow.

The second crucial topic we will consider in this chapter is that Genesis's authors, the Storyteller and the Priest, select Noah as the founder of their family. He is their founding ancestor, the ancestor who defined their own identity and the size and shape of their family. This point is *very* controversial. It's controversial because Genesis's interpreters have universally given this title to Abraham. They identify Abraham as Israel's founding father, the ancestor who defined Israel's identity and the shape of its family. This viewpoint has not only carried the day in biblical scholarship but also determined the way readers of Genesis have understood Israel's identity and its relationship to others. It has determined the way readers understand the biblical view of difference. So before we can pursue the controversial claim that Noah defines Israel and its family, and the consequences of this claim for understanding difference, we acknowledge the counterclaim that Abraham is Israel's founding father. Because this is how everyone thinks today, it presents us with some challenging ways of understanding identity and difference in Genesis.

Abraham's Ambiguous Legacy

Abraham is a giant figure who dominates the landscape of Genesis in numerous ways. He is a righteous man who obeys God and becomes God's covenant partner (Gen 15, 17). At God's command, he moves to the land that would become biblical Israel (Gen 12:1-7). He receives promises of land, descendants, nationhood, and blessing for himself and his descendants, promises that are repeated to his son, Isaac, and his grandson, Jacob, after him (Gen 12:1-3; 26:3-5; 28:13-14). He is one of Israel's most vividly remembered ancestors. The Storyteller and the Priest preserve

---

2. Sarsour, "Linda Sarsour," 283.

extended collections of traditions about Abraham's life and family (Gen 12–25). And he leads many lists of Israel's ancestors, when biblical authors refer to Israel as the descendants of Abraham, Isaac, and Jacob (e.g., Exod 3:16; Deut 6:10).

Eventually Judaism, Christianity, and Islam (the three great religions that emerged from these scriptural traditions) each adopted Abraham as their founding ancestor.[3] In Judaism, Abraham became known as "the father of the Jewish people . . . the founder of Judaism itself—the first Jew, as it were—and the man whose life in some mysterious ways pre-enacts the experience of the Jewish people."[4] Today the Jewish liturgy refers to God as "the God of Abraham, the God of Isaac, and the God of Jacob." The Christian apostle Paul saw in Abraham the father of the community of faith that came into being with Jesus Christ: "That's why the inheritance comes through faith, so that it will be on the basis of God's grace," writes Paul. "In that way, the promise is secure for all Abraham's descendants, not just for those who are related by Law but also for those who are related by the faith of Abraham, who is the father of us all" (Rom 4:16). Indeed, the author of Matthew's Gospel begins Jesus's own lineage with Abraham (Matt 1:1-2). Islam regards Abraham as "the ideal precursor of the pure monotheism that is Islam . . . the ideal precursor of Muhammad."[5] Abraham and his son, Ishmael, construct the house of God at Mecca.

Because Judaism, Christianity, and Islam trace their origins back to Abraham as their founding father, Abraham became a strong unifying symbol for members of these religious traditions when the American Muslim community experienced fear, hate, and mistreatment from other Americans after the events of 9/11. Since a founding ancestor defines not just the identity of

---

3. Jon D. Levenson, *Inheriting Abraham: The Legacy of the Patriarch in Judaism, Christianity, and Islam* (Princeton, NJ: Princeton University Press, 2012).

4. Levenson, *Inheriting Abraham*, 3.

5. Roberto Tottoli, "Abraham," in *Biblical Prophets in the Qur'ān and Muslim Literature* (Richmond, Great Britain: Curzon, 2002), 26–27.

his descendants but also the extent of their family, all three religions, by appealing to Abraham, could claim membership in a single family. As members of the same family, they could find a language for their relationship and a way of understanding their solidarity with one another in the midst of their differences and of new tensions and conflicts. This power of a founding ancestor to create a sense of solidarity among his descendants is an important dynamic we will explore in a moment. After 9/11, membership in one family provided a way of thinking that brought members of different religions together to engage each other, to talk about their unique experiences, and to negotiate their differences.

At the same time, there are limitations, both modern and ancient, in using the figure of Abraham as a founding ancestor and unifying figure. For contemporary religious communities, Abraham provides a common forefather for Judaism, Christianity, and Islam—however different their views of him might be— and a way to think about what their own kinship relationships to each other as members of his single family might look like. At the same time, Abraham's family tree does not include members of the other religious communities of the world. So, while Abraham's family includes three great religions and provides a kinship context for talking about their relationships, it excludes at the same time most of the world, the members of all other religions. It separates those inside the family of Abraham from those outside of it.

For ancient Israel, in a similar way, viewing Abraham as the founding ancestor situates Israel in a very small family in ancient West Asia. This ancient family includes, together with Jacob/ Israel, Israel's nearest and specific ancestor, the ancestors of the Ishmaelites, Ammonites, Moabites, and Edomites, Israel's closest neighbors. This is a very small part of Israel's ancient world, a tiny lineage among all the lineages of the great family tree that the Storyteller and the Priest construct in the book of Genesis. Starting with Abraham thus gives ancient Israel a limited and exclusive genealogical identity within its larger world, creating a small group of insiders and a very large world of outsiders.

The selection of Abraham by Judaism, Christianity, and Islam as their founding ancestor has profoundly influenced our reading of Genesis. Most modern scholars, just as most interpreters through history, have adopted this claim as the key to reading the book of Genesis. These interpreters regard Abraham as Israel's founding ancestor and the pivotal figure in the book of Genesis. This influences their understanding of the book, its architecture, its aim, and its meaning. And, for our purposes in particular, it influences their understanding of Israel's identity and its view of difference. By reading Genesis with Abraham as its center, Genesis's interpreters have advanced a view of Israelite identity that sharply restricts the boundaries of its own family and also, as we will see, distinguishes Israel from others in ways that its authors did not intend to do.

Here is how most of Genesis's interpreters have used Abraham to project such a view of Israel's sense of its own identity and its attitude toward difference in the book of Genesis. In the first place, by limiting Israel's genealogical identity to the descendants of Abraham alone, they have given Israel, as we have just noted, a very small family of belonging within its larger world. In the second place, they have used Abraham to distinguish Israel from others in several significant ways. They have accomplished this by dividing the pre-Abrahamic era of their history sharply from the post-Abrahamic era. Genesis's interpreters have contrasted these eras before and after Abraham in four consequential ways.

First, they portray the age before Abraham as the era of universal humanity, and the age after Abraham as the era of Israelite history proper, thus dividing Israelite history into non-Israelite and Israelite ages and removing Israel from the larger flow of world history. Second, and this is true only of contemporary scholars who have invented this terminology, such scholars portray the age of universal humanity before Abraham as a mythic world and the age of Israelite history after Abraham as a historical world full of the realities of antiquity, thus granting Israel a more authentic space in "actual" history. Third, they portray the age of universal humanity before Abraham as an era under God's curse and the age after Abraham of Israelite history proper as an era of God's blessing, thus distinguishing Israelites as blessed from others who are not. Finally, and most important of all for our thinking about identity and difference, Genesis's interpreters portray the age of universal humanity before Abraham as an era of disobedience and sinfulness and the age of Israelite history proper after Abraham as an era of obedience and righteousness.

According to this traditional scheme, the age before Abraham is a mythical era of universal humanity that descends into sin and comes under God's curse. By contrast, the age after Abraham is an historical era of Israel proper, in which Israel's own ancestors are obedient and righteous and live in God's blessing. To advance this way of reading Genesis and the views of identity and difference that accompany it, scholars divide the book of Genesis into these two parts, the ages before and after Abraham. Many even write commentaries on Genesis in two volumes, the before-Abraham volume of Genesis 1–11 and the after-Abraham volume of Genesis 12–50.[6] All have chosen Abraham as Israel's founding ancestor, and that has made all the difference.

This is the ambiguous legacy of Abraham that we have been given for reading Genesis. And like the legacy of interpretation of the Babel story, this way of reading Genesis also presents us with some problematic ways of thinking about identity and difference.

---

6. Here is a list of some of them. Claus Westermann, *Genesis 1–11*, trans. John J. Scullion (Minneapolis: Augsburg, 1984); Donald E. Gowan, From *Eden to Babel: Genesis 1–11* (Grand Rapids, MI: Eerdmans, 1988); Terence E. Fretheim, *Creation, Fall, and Flood: Studies in Genesis 1–11* (Minneapolis: Augsburg, 1969); Conrad L'Heureux, *In and Out of Paradise: The Book of Genesis from Adam and Eve to the Tower of Babel* (New York: Paulist, 1983); Isaac M. Kikawada and Arthur Quinn, *Before Abraham Was: The Unity of Genesis 1–11* (Nashville: Abingdon Press, 1985); Ellen van Wolde, *Words Become Worlds: Semantic Studies of Genesis 1–11* (Leiden: Brill, 1994); Richard D. Nelson, *From Eden to Babel: An Adventure in Bible Study* (St. Louis: Chalice, 2006).

It separates Israel and its identity sharply from the diverse world around it. And it distinguishes Israelite identity from others in ways that Genesis authors did not intend to do, and that represents a strongly exclusivist reading of Genesis. It defines Israel's primary distinctives in Genesis as a special historical authenticity, as a unique claim to righteousness, and as an exclusive possession of blessing, which are all characteristics absent in others.

This is the powerful way of reading Genesis that we have all shared for centuries. It is the reading that we will now reconsider by exploring the claim that Israel's great epic writers, the Storyteller and the Priest, actually chose Noah as their founding ancestor. And by selecting Noah, they provide us with a completely different understanding of identity and difference, an understanding that was much more generous and constructive for them in their world, and that can be so for us in our world today.

Dividing History

In his studies of how societies remember and shape their past to locate themselves in the world and express their identity, Eviatar Zerubavel gives us a model for understanding how scholars have represented Israel's history in Genesis and also for how we can rethink it. This model is the common practice among societies of telling their history as discontinuous.[7] Constructing a discontinuous vision of the past involves two basic strategies. The first is identifying a watershed event that breaks history into discrete chapters or periods. Such a watershed event is presented as a sharp break in the flow of history, a turning point in the past that brings one era to a close and launches another. The second strategy is attributing separate and uniform identities to the periods before and after such a watershed event. This second strategy

---

7. Eviatar Zerubavel, *Time Maps: Collective Memory and the Social Shape of the Past* (Chicago: University of Chicago Press, 2003), 82–100.

includes both "intraperiodic lumping," as Zerubavel calls it, which involves exaggerating the uniformity within a period, and "interperiodic splitting," which involves exaggerating the dissimilarity between the two periods. The past is thereby remembered as discontinuous: two distinct and uniform periods separated by a single defining moment.

Periodizing history is not an objective representation of the facts, of course, but a social construct that a society imposes on its actual history to wrest meaning from it. Framing its history as discontinuous is undertaken, as Zerubavel shows, to help a society articulate its cultural, political, and moral identity.[8] By dividing its history and locating its beginnings in a watershed event, a society makes an explicit claim about its understanding of itself and its relationship to other societies around it. This turning point marks the end of some prior cultural reality in the period preceding it, and it signals the beginning of a new group identity in the period following it. Most Protestants, for example, claim that the Reformation began with Martin Luther in 1517, rather than with other Reformers before or after. They characterize the era before Luther as an age of a false, or inadequate, or, at least, a different religious consciousness, and they describe themselves, Luther's true heirs, as beginning a new era of religious consciousness. Similar turning points in history are embraced by subsequent followers of Reformers in other territories, such as the founders John Calvin or John Wesley.

This is precisely the kind of periodizing of history and identity construction that the Bible's interpreters have attributed to the authors of Genesis. To claim Abraham as the pivotal event or figure in Israel's early history and as the defining moment of Israel's identity, most of Genesis's interpreters have argued, as we have seen, that Genesis's authors presented the periods before and after Abraham as individually homogenous and distinctly different from one another. We can agree with Genesis's interpreters

---

8. Zerubavel, *Time Maps*, 84–85.

that the Storyteller and the Priest, like historians in many other cultures, divided their history to give it meaning and to articulate their identity. But we will discover that Genesis's authors periodized their early history differently from the way that their interpreters think they did, and, consequently, that they created a different view of their identity and their relation to others than their interpreters have.

In the pages that follow, we will explore the same biblical evidence that interpreters have used to identify Abraham as the great watershed in Genesis, but we will see that this evidence actually points to Noah, not to Abraham, as the defining moment in biblical history. Both the Storyteller and the Priest make Noah, not Abraham, the pivotal figure in their history, dividing their past into two distinct periods. They claim that Noah was their founding ancestor who defined their identity and the shape of their family. We will also discover that by the way they divided history with their founding ancestor Noah and by the way they characterized the periods before and after him, Genesis's authors constructed a different understanding of themselves, their place in the world, and their relationship to others than their interpreters thought they did. By starting their lineage with Noah, the Storyteller and the Priest were able to firmly embrace and ground their own identity in their diverse world, and they were also able to understand themselves in genuine relationships to the diverse peoples around them.

Noah and the Great Flood

By far, the greatest break in biblical history is the great flood, when all life perishes, except the lives on Noah's great ship, after which everything begins over again. Completely. So, it is simple common sense to wonder whether the Storyteller and the Priest, who both preserved traditions about the great flood, thought of the flood and its hero Noah as the great watershed moment in their history, the event that divided their past into two different ages. In fact, the great Mesopotamian civilizations to Israel's east, the very place where the Storyteller located the Babel story and the origin of Israel's own ancestors (Gen 11:9; 15:7), had their own flood traditions. According to these traditions, the flood marked their own history's decisive break.

In the Sumerian King List, the continuous dynastic succession of kingships founded at the creation of the world is interrupted by a great flood, so that kingship has to be lowered a second time from heaven after the flood, just as it had been at creation. Kish, the first royal city after the flood, founds the first true Sumerian city-state and the new power of kingship associated with it. This first post-flood city-state created such a powerful new royal identity for the Sumerians that later Mesopotamian kings took the title "King of Kish."[9] In the Atraḫasis Epic, unchecked reproduction and rampant population growth characterize the first age of history, which the great flood brings to an end. To control population and stabilize the world after the flood, new measures of birth control are instituted: sterile women unable to reproduce, the *pashittu* demon who snatches babies from their mothers and thus ensures high infant mortality rates, and women serving priestly functions who don't marry and have children. Here too the flood introduces a new social identity: human reproduction governed by severe constraints, the very constraints that defined the author's own world.[10]

Israel's own historians, the Storyteller and the Priest, like their ancient counterparts, actually believe that the flood is the decisive

---

9. Thorkild Jacobsen, *The Sumerian King List* (Chicago: University of Chicago Press, 1939), 155. H. W. F. Saggs, *The Greatness That Was Babylon* (New York: New American Library, 1962), 54–60.

10. William L. Moran, "Atraḫasis: The Babylonian Story of the Flood," Biblica 52 (1971): 51–61; Tikva Frymer-Kensky, "The Atraḫasis Epic and Its Significance for Our Understanding of Genesis 1–9," *Biblical Archeologist* (December 1977): 147–55; A. D. Kilmer, "The Mesopotamian Concept of Overpopulation and Its Solution as Reflected in Mythology," *Orentalia* 41 (1972): 160–77.

break in their own history. They think of their flood hero Noah as the pivotal figure in their history and in their ancestry. They describe Noah as the figure that divides their history into two very different historical periods. And they consider Noah to be their founding ancestor, who defines their own identity and who determines the shape and size of their family. They write their history to claim Noah as their founding ancestor, rather than Abraham, as their later interpreters did. And claiming Noah as their ancestor has a profound influence on the way they understand their own ethnic identity and on the way they understand their relationship to those with other ethnic identities. Claiming Noah as their founding ancestor has everything to do with their view of difference.

Noah Founds Israel's Family

One of the four arguments that the majority of Genesis's interpreters have made to claim that Abraham is Israel's founding ancestor is that Abraham divided Israel's history by ending an age of universal humanity (Gen 1–11) and introducing the age of Israel and its specific cultural identity (Gen 12–50).[11] This claim is as puzzling as it is widespread, because both the Storyteller and the Priest describe the history before Abraham in very concrete and specific details as their own history. They thus follow the common practice that societies don't describe their origins in universal terms but within their own particular cultural horizon. From the account of the creation of the world itself, down to Abraham's own generation, they tell history with the concrete details of their

---

11. Representatives of this widely held view include Nahum Sarna, *Genesis* (Philadelphia: Jewish Publication Society, 1989), 84–85; and Walter Brueggemann, *Genesis* (Atlanta: John Knox, 1982), 116–17. Other statements of this approach may be found in Westermann, *Genesis 1–11*, 2–4, 600, 606; Jon Levenson, "The Universal Horizon of Biblical Particularism," in *Ethnicity and the Bible*, ed. Mark G. Brett (Leiden: Brill, 1996), 147; and in Jonathan Sacks, *The Dignity of Difference: How to Avoid the Clash of Civilizations* (London: Continuum, 2002), 50–51.

own unique land, economy, family structures, and religious experience. They tell history from the outset not as a generic human history but as the history of their own beginnings.

The Storyteller, for example, portrays his earliest ancestors—Adam, Cain, and Noah—not as universal humans at all but as typical Israelite farmers, practicing the subsistence rain-fed agriculture of the Israelite highlands and not, for example, the irrigation agriculture of the great river valley civilizations of Mesopotamia and Egypt (Gen 2:5; cf. Deut 11:10-11). They participate in Israel's own mixed agricultural economy, cultivating the grains that are the staple of highland agriculture (Gen 2:5; 3:18-19), supplementing them with the fruits from their vineyards and orchards (2:9; 8:11; 9:20), and raising flocks of sheep and goats (4:1-2).[12] These stories reflect the world of subsistence agriculture in the Mediterranean highlands of ancient Israel, in which the Storyteller grew up.

The Priest's early history is just as indigenous and particularly Israelite. In his creation narrative (Gen 1:1–2:4a), the Priest grounds the key features of Israel's religious ritual at the beginning of time. God creates the world in a week to sanctify the Israelite Sabbath on the seventh day and to ground it in the orders of creation (Gen 2:1-4a; Exod 20:8-11; 31:12-17). God creates the heavenly bodies to mark the beginning and end of Israel's "sacred seasons," the great festivals in Israel's own liturgical calendar (Gen 1:14; Lev 23). Like the Storyteller, the Priest locates creation within Israel's own agricultural landscape. He categorizes the plants God creates on the third day according to the two major crops—grains producing visible seeds, and fruits with their seeds inside them—raised by Israelite farmers (Gen 1:11-12).[13] Using precise formulae, terminology, and literary patterns, the

---

12. Theodore Hiebert, *The Yahwist's Landscape: Nature and Religion in Early Israel* (New York: Oxford, 1996), 30–82.

13. Theodore Hiebert, "Biblical Perspectives on Biodiversity: A Conversation with E. O. Wilson," in *The Old Testament in the Life of God's People*, ed. Jon Isaak (Winona Lake, IN: Eisenbrauns, 2009), 269–81, esp. pp. 277–78.

Priest links the creation of the world in Genesis 1 closely with his later description of the construction of the wilderness sanctuary in Exodus 36–40, so that in the Priest's history, the created world and the wilderness sanctuary mirror each other.[14] The Priest's pre-flood generations, just as the Storyteller's, are Israel's own ancestors, practicing Israelite religion and farming on its own soil.

Both the Storyteller and Priest frame their own early history at the beginning of Genesis as a genealogy of their family. They present their history as a family history, documenting each generation of their own ancestry since the beginning of time (Gen 4:1-2, 17-25; 5:1-32). This language of family and kinship, as we have already recognized, will be the lens through which they view their history, their own identity, and their relationship to others throughout the book of Genesis. In their account of their family's past, they recognize a decisive break in their genealogical history. For the Storyteller and the Priest, this sharp break occurs in Noah's generation at the flood, not much later in Abraham's generation. Before the flood, both the Storyteller and the Priest document Israel's family history by unilinear genealogies, which are genealogies that describe one line of descent from father to son. The Storyteller, for example, traces his first ancestors from the first man to Cain to Enoch to Irad, and so on (4:17-24). The Priest traces his descent from Adam to Seth to Enosh to Kenan, and so on (5:1-32). Unilinear genealogies like this are intended to document a culture's own particular family and its history.

But after the flood in Noah's generation, everything changes. Both the Storyteller and the Priest begin to tell their history with segmented genealogies. Segmented genealogies are branched genealogies with more than one line of descent. A segmented genealogy is, in fact, a family tree. It includes not only one descendant but several descendants or branches and then their several

14. Joseph Blenkinsopp, "The Structure of P," *Catholic Biblical Quarterly* 38 (1976): 275–83; William P. Brown, *The Ethos of the Cosmos: The Genesis of Moral Imagination in the Bible* (Grand Rapids, MI: Eerdmans, 1999), 73–74.

descendants and branches and so on. So, for example, Noah's three sons, Shem, Ham, and Japheth, become the three great branches from whom their own children branch out and from whom branch out eventually the ancestors of all the peoples of the world. Noah's family tree is the world's family tree. And the ancestors of Israel, from Shem through a series of his descendants, become one small branch in this great global family tree. Abraham is not the founder of this great complex ancestry of which Israel becomes a part. He is simply the third to the last generation before Israel/Jacob, whose sons become the tribes of Israel. Noah founds the grand family in which Israel is a single lineage.

By shifting to segmented genealogies after the flood, both the Storyteller and the Priest shift their attention from their own exclusive pedigree before the flood to their place within the larger family of peoples and nations after the flood. Thus, if we are to talk of the relationship between Israel in particular and humanity in general at the beginning of Genesis, it is only after the flood—not before it—that humanity in its true breadth really comes into view. The flood provides the pivot from the Storyteller's and the Priest's documentation of their own specific origins to their documentation of their place within and their relationship to humanity as a whole in the world's family tree anchored by Noah. In their post-flood genealogies, the Storyteller and the Priest provide a cultural map of the entire world and the exact location of Israel within that world as they understood it.

Having established Noah as the trunk of Israel's family tree, we are in a position to talk about how choosing Noah as their founding ancestor, rather than Abraham, expresses Genesis's authors understanding of their own identity and their relation to others. Let's begin with Israel's claims about its own identity and its own standing in the world. By starting their history with Noah, rather than with Abraham, Genesis's authors make the strongest possible claim for their own status and legitimacy. In the world of genealogies, depth equals status. "Like foundations of buildings, pedigrees seem more solid the 'deeper' they go," writes Zerubavel. "In order to enhance our stature and legitimacy, we therefore try to stretch our pedigrees back as far as we can."[15] As Howard Bloch puts it, "antiquity is lineage's chief claim to legitimacy; and the older the genealogy, the more prestigious and powerful that claim becomes."[16]

By starting their history with Noah, the Storyteller and the Priest give their own ethnic identity the strongest possible legitimacy and status, equal to any other of Noah's lineages, that is, equal to any other people. Just as Mesopotamian kings gave their legitimacy as much depth as possible by tracing their lineage to Kish, the first royal city after the flood, so both the Storyteller and the Priest enhance their status by tracing their ancestry all the way back to Noah, their flood hero, the ancestor of all peoples. They express the same pride in their distinctive ethnicity that the people of Babel did in the ethnic identity they set about creating after the great flood. By contrast, Genesis's interpreters have greatly reduced Israel's status by dividing history at Abraham and by starting Israel's ancestry proper with a much later and more recent ancestor.

In addition to making a much stronger claim to their own status in the world, by beginning their history with Noah rather than Abraham, Genesis's authors also make a broader, more extensive, and more inclusive claim about their relationships to others. By identifying Noah as their first ancestor, they select as their primary family the largest possible kinship group—the world's family, so to speak. Genealogies play two roles. They establish the depth of a people's identity, and thereby its status, but they also establish its breadth, and thereby the size of its family or community. Descent equals co-descent. This is one reason why millions of families are sifting contact information from thousands of cousins

---

15. Eviatar Zerubavel, *Ancestors and Relatives: Genealogy, Identity, and Community* (Oxford: Oxford University Press, 2011), 78–79.

16. R. Howard Bloch, *Etymologies and Genealogies: A Literary Anthropology of the French Middle Ages* (Chicago: University of Chicago Press, 1983), 84.

through DNA matching. "Genealogies," writes Zerubavel, "are two-dimensional mental structures whose breadth is directly proportional to their depth.... The further back we go in search of our ancestors, the greater number of 'relatives' we are likely to identify, and the more inclusive our genealogical identity is therefore likely to be."[17] Both the Storyteller and the Priest construct for Israel the most inclusive genealogical identity possible.

By beginning their lineage with Noah, the most fundamental identity claim Genesis's authors make for their Israelite culture is that they are members of the entire human family and related to all branches of it. Both the Storyteller and the Priest position themselves as a branch in the same family to which all others belong, not as a people outside that family. This is the point Frank Crüsemann recognized when he wrote of Israel's self-definition in the genealogical system of Genesis: "Israel has written itself into the world of peoples...the necessary divisions are described, and the aim is undoubtedly the origin of Israel. But who this Israel is can only be grasped within the framework as a whole; the ethnic group is part of the entire coherence of humanity."[18] By contrast, the majority of Genesis's interpreters, by starting with Abraham, provide Israel a much more exclusive genealogical identity, limiting Israel's membership to the family composed of the very small and recent lineage of Abraham's descendants alone, including their closest neighbors, the Ishmaelites, Moabites, Ammonites, and Edomites. For Genesis's interpreters, therefore, the bulk of humanity lies outside Israel's family.

In addition to selecting humanity as their family by making Noah their founding ancestor, Genesis's authors emphasize their intrinsic relationship to all the lineages in their extensive family. This is the purpose of family trees. Thus, the fundamental identity claim that Genesis's authors make is that all other peoples

---

17. Eviatar Zerubavel, *Ancestors and Relatives*, 37, 51.

18. Frank Crüsemann, "Human Solidarity and Ethnic Identity: Israel's Self-Definition in the Genealogical System of Genesis," in *Ethnicity and the Bible*, ed. Mark Brett (Leiden: Brill, 1996), 58, 66.

are their relatives. They view their relations to others through the lens of family relationships. As Zerubavel states, genealogies are above all "visions of relatedness."[19] In his most recent reflections on the nature of kinship, Marshal Sahlins identifies its core quality as "mutuality of being: kinfolk are persons who participate intrinsically in each other's existence, they are members of one another."[20]

Finally, by starting their history at the flood and locating themselves within the family of Noah and its various lineages, Genesis's authors construct a less binary and a much more sophisticated, complex, and nuanced view of others and of their relationships to them than many of Genesis's interpreters have recognized. Genealogies are designed to measure and claim degrees of kinship, differences between the more distant relatives early in a lineage and closer relatives who emerge later. In genealogical constructions of history, therefore, there is no universal Other or single Not I, but a myriad of images of those who inhabit different but related lineages. In their post-flood genealogies and genealogical narratives, the Storyteller and the Priest paint a multifaceted picture of Israel's varied relationships with the peoples of their world, recognizing various distances, tensions, conflicts, alliances, covenants, kinships, and histories that make each one of their relationships with others distinctive and unique. By contrast, Genesis's interpreters have described a simpler binary relationship between Israel and the Other. By emphasizing the divide between Abraham's family and the rest of humanity, they have created in general a strongly homogenous image of the non-Israelite.

To summarize, by choosing Noah as their founding ancestor, the Storyteller and the Priest embrace both their own ethnic identity and their relationship with other ethnicities more strongly than many of Genesis's interpreters have led us to believe. By using

---

19. Zerubavel, *Ancestors and Relatives*, ix.
20. Marshal Sahlins, *What Kinship Is—And Is Not* (Chicago: University of Chicago Press, 2013), ix.

the language of family to articulate their relationships to other peoples, Genesis's authors have made them all family and have claimed them as relatives. Their starting point for thinking about others is the deep primal experience of family. The Storyteller and the Priest inhabited a world that was, to use Linda Sarsour's words, "a place where families and neighbors were one in the same." All other ethnicities are part of the family. They are branches of the same tree. According to this way of thinking about difference, difference is real but always related in some way to one's own identity. Difference is always perceived within an underlying sense of relationship. And it is this sense of relationship that provides a primal way to begin thinking about difference and engaging it.

Noah Founds Israel's World

Genesis's interpreters have claimed three other contrasts in the periods of Israel's history before and after Abraham in order to divide Israel's history at Abraham and to make Abraham Israel's founding ancestor. And all three claims have made distinctions between Israel and others unintended by the authors of Genesis. One of these claims is a very modern idea. This is the claim that the age before Abraham in Genesis 1–11 is a mythic era and that the age after Abraham in Genesis 12–50 is a historical era full of the names of real places and peoples. Abraham therefore begins Israelite history proper.[21] This is a very popular way of reading Genesis today. Before we even reexamine the evidence for this distinction in Genesis itself, however, we must face up to two preliminary problems. The first is the fact that ancient authors didn't make this distinction between myth and history, so we can hardly

---

21. See, for example, Hermann Gunkel, *The Legends of Genesis* (New York: Schocken Books, 1964), 14; Gunkel, *Genesis*, trans. Mark Biddle (Macon, GA: Mercer University Press, 1997), xiii; William F. Albright, *Yahweh and the Gods of Canaan* (Winona Lake, IN: Eisenbrauns, 1968), 53–109; Sarna, *Genesis*, xiv; and Brueggemann, *Genesis*, 11. The Israel Museum places the patriarchs in a specific historical period, the Middle Bronze Age.

attribute to them such a contrast. The second problem is that contemporary scholars themselves don't share a common definition of "myth," nor do they agree on the actual "historical" character of the narratives in Genesis. So, it is very hard to find any contemporary consensus on how to differentiate between myth and history in these two ages.

Since Genesis's authors didn't make the modern distinction between "myth" and "history," and since Genesis's recent interpreters do not themselves agree about what they mean by such a distinction, we might argue for simply abandoning this kind of evidence for Abraham as history's pivotal figure and Israel's founding ancestor. However, when we reexamine the details of Israel's early history in Genesis, we do notice an actual shift in the kinds of political realities that Genesis's authors describe. This shift may actually be partly responsible for the modern introduction of the ideas of myth and history. But this shift occurs at the flood with Noah rather than with Abraham. We might describe this shift as one from a pre-flood age of real cultural realities but without concrete political identifications to a post-flood age in which peoples and places do have concrete political and geographical identifications, something like the shift we also see occurring in the Sumerian King List.

As we have already seen, Israel's ancestors before the flood live in the real and particular world of Mediterranean highland agriculture and within the Israelite religious ritual that the Storyteller and Priest themselves knew. Yet none of the places and cultural realities before the flood—the Garden of Eden, the farm on which Cain and Abel lived, the desert (the land of Nod) to which Cain was expelled (Gen 4:16), the first city (Gen 4:17), or Lamech's residence—can be identified with any specific, concrete places or events of Israel's own world, that is, with the political realities of antiquity.

In the genealogical narratives of Noah's family following the flood, however, the actual political entities and realities of Israel and its larger world come into view immediately. The Storyteller's first episode after the flood, the story of the curse on Canaan (9:18-27), identifies the ancestor of the actual place (Canaan) and people (Canaanites) from which Israel itself emerged at the end of the second and beginning of the first millennium BCE. Furthermore, the Storyteller's and the Priest's genealogical traditions following the flood describe the origins of other actual peoples and places from the known world, starting with Gomer, the *gimmiraya* of Mesopotamian cuneiform sources, and including the peoples and cities of Greece and Asia Minor (10:2-4), Egypt, northern Africa, Arabia (10:6-7, 13-14), Mesopotamia (10:8-12), and the Canaanites, Hittites, and Syrians (10:14-19), to name just some of the major examples.[22] The Storyteller's account of Babel that follows these genealogies explains not just the name of this important ancient city but also how the world's cultures spread out from it (11:1-9).

Noah, therefore, founds not only Israel's family but its real world. Within his family tree emerge all the real peoples and political realities, which filled the world of the Storyteller and the Priest and within which their own ethnic identity as a small West Asian kingdom was formed. As one of the many lineages of Noah that make up the peoples of the world in which Israel lives, Israel shares the same political space and the common political realities of all Noah's descendants. The Storyteller and the Priest both focus in much more detail on their own lineage among all Noah's descendants, but they do not set their own lineage apart in any way that grants them more historical veracity than any other people. Claiming Noah as the founder of their world in no way grants Israel a less "mythical" status in the real political landscape they inhabited. The Storyteller and Priest both see their own ethnic culture sharing equally the world of ethnic cultures that emerges from Noah's descendants.

---

22. Sarna provides a helpful, brief survey in *Genesis,* 67–80.

Noah Founds a Righteous World

By far the most important distinction Genesis's interpreters claim to see in the ages before and after Abraham in order to make Abraham the pivotal figure in Israel's history and Israel's founding ancestor is the distinction between sin and righteousness.[23] Unlike the modern distinction between myth and history, this is a very old claim, one Genesis's interpreters have made from the very beginning of the history of interpretation of Genesis. According to this claim, everyone before Abraham failed to obey God and to live righteous lives. Even after the flood, which was God's attempt to punish earth's evildoers and to start over, sin multiplied and became entrenched in the human race. So God gave up on humanity. Only by selecting a single small family, the family of Abraham, out of all the sinful families of the world, could God ensure the existence of righteousness on the earth. Of the contrasts Genesis's interpreters have claimed before and after Abraham, this distinction is the sharpest and most significant, since it divides righteous Israel from an unrighteous humanity.

Both the Storyteller and the Priest indeed thought their own earliest ancestors sinned. But both also believed Noah, rather than Abraham, changed things completely. Both writers portray their founding ancestor Noah as the world's first righteous man and the founder of a righteous age of history. Let's begin with the Storyteller's version of Israel's early history. In it, the first couple disobeys God's command in the Garden of Eden (Gen 2:17; 3:11-13, 16-19), and then their son, Cain, disobeys God's command to resist sin before he kills his brother (4:7, 10-13). The pre-flood generation that follows is thoroughly evil (6:5-7). But Noah, unlike his predecessors, is obedient and does everything

---

23. Forceful statements of the contrast between sin and righteousness in these parts of Genesis, by way of example, may be found in Claus Westermann, *Genesis 1–11*, 66, and *Genesis 12–36*, trans. John J. Scullion (Minneapolis: Augsburg, 1985), 27; Brueggemann, *Genesis*, 106; Sarna, *Genesis*, 85–90; Levenson, *Inheriting Abraham*, 18–19; and Bill T. Arnold, *Genesis* (Cambridge: Cambridge University Press, 2009), 126.

God commands him (7:5). He is righteous (7:1) and finds favor in God's eyes (6:5). Abraham also is obedient (12:4), righteous (15:6; 18:19), and finds favor in God's eyes (18:3), but in so doing, he simply reflects the righteousness of his ancestor Noah. According to the Storyteller, Noah build's Israel's first altar and thereby establishes its core religious rituals (8:20), an act later repeated by both Abraham and Isaac (12:7, 8; 13:18; 26:25).

The primary obstacle to understanding Noah and his descendants as beginning the new age of righteousness has always been the Storyteller's account of Babel after the flood (11:1-9). But we now know that the story of Babel does not describe an arrogant attack on God and God's rule but is an account of the creation of human culture after the flood and then of God's decision to diversify the world's cultures. Nor should we consider the story of Noah's vineyard (9:20-27) a new outbreak of sin. Many interpreters have considered Noah's wine drinking sinful, but the story itself describes Noah's behavior neutrally and without censure, as recent scholars have recognized.[24] The aim of this story is to censure Ham's behavior, and by extension, in particular, Canaan's, but this is the single, precise, and purposeful exception to the Storyteller's portrayal of Noah and Noah's age as righteous. Censuring Canaan has a particular purpose, to which we will return in the next chapter.

Like the Storyteller, the Priest views Noah rather than Abraham as the moral turning point in the book of Genesis. The Priest's pre-flood accounts of creation (1:1–2:4a) and of the world's first generations (5:1-28, 30-32) make no mention of disobedience and sin, but the Priest does think the pre-flood era became filled with evil. By the time of the flood, every living thing had become corrupt (6:11, 12) and the earth was filled with violence and lawlessness (6:11, 13). Like the Storyteller, the Priest presents

---

24. Arnold, *Genesis*, 112; Brueggemann, *Genesis*, 89. Neither the author of *Jubilees* (7:1-8) nor Josephus (*Antiquities* 1.6.3) viewed Noah's drinking negatively. Translators render the phrase "they drank together and were at ease" positively in Gen 43:34 (NRSV: "were merry;" NJPS: "drank their fill") but negatively in Gen 9:21 (NRSV, NJPS: "became drunk").

his founding ancestor Noah as the world's first righteous figure. In the Priest's eyes, Noah is morally flawless (6:9) and walks with God (6:9).[25] He is righteous (6:9) and obedient, doing exactly as God commands him (6:22; 7:9, 16; 8:18). These traits are the same marks of righteousness the Priest later attributes to Abraham. Indeed, when God later *commands* Abraham to walk before God and to be blameless (17:1), the Priest leaves the impression that Abraham is to emulate Noah, the first person to possess these traits. Like Noah, the Priest's Abraham is obedient, doing just as God says (17:23; 21:4).

In two other ways the Priest identifies Noah, rather than Abraham, as the moral turning point in Genesis and the founder of the world's righteous age. First, the Priest applies to Noah for the first time in Israelite history what Joseph Blenkinsopp calls an "execution formula," a formula the Priest uses for persons faithfully executing divine commands.[26] The Priest uses this formula originally to describe Noah's construction of the ark (6:22), and then he uses it at other key moments in Israel's history: Abraham's circumcision of the men in his household (17:23), Moses's and Aaron's mission to Pharaoh (Exod 7:6), the Israelites' first observation of Passover (12:28), and Moses's and the Israelites' construction of the meeting tent (or tabernacle) (39:32), to mention just a few important instances. When the Priest links Noah's construction of the ark to Moses's construction of the meeting tent—the only two instances where the Priest uses this execution formula for objects built according to divine specifications—the Priest identifies Noah as the founder of his religious history that culminates in the climactic events of God's encounter with Israel

---

25. Enoch, the seventh member of the Priest's primeval generations, also walked with God, but the Priest calls him neither righteous nor blameless (Gen 5:22-24). Furthermore, the Priest's tradition that God "took" him is likely a euphemism for death, to explain his short life span, rather than an attempt to attribute to him any special righteousness (Sarna, *Genesis*, 43). Of course, later interpreters increased his status, as the apocryphal works in his name attest.

26. Blenkinsopp, "The Structure of P," 275–77, 283–86.

at Mount Sinai.[27] It was at Mount Sinai that the religious legislation governing Priestly ritual and life was fully introduced.

Finally, the Priest transforms the world's moral landscape in Noah's time by casting Noah as God's first covenant partner. The covenant is the primary organizing feature by which the Priest divides Israel's history, separating Israelite history into the ages of Noah (Gen 9:1-17), of Abraham (17:1-27), and of Moses and the Israelites at Sinai (Exod 31:12-18), God's three covenant partners. This covenantal structure points to Noah rather than Abraham as history's pivotal figure, since Noah represents the beginning of covenantal history. In the age of sin before the flood, Israel's earliest ancestors lacked a covenant relationship with God, and this age devolved into corruption and lawlessness. In the new age following the flood, God builds a secure link to Noah and Noah's descendants by covenants. The Priest's covenantal age thus begins in the covenant with Noah and all Noah's descendants. The covenants with Abraham and with Israel at Mount Sinai further specify the nature of the unique relationship between God and Israel's own particular lineage within this larger covenant, but they do not initiate the covenantal era. Noah does.

God's covenant with Noah introduces the world's first priestly legislation regulating human behavior, a means by which God places the world on a new moral footing after the flood.[28] This legislation aims to curb the lawlessness and violence of the pre-flood world by protecting the sanctity of life. Its stipulations prohibit the consumption of blood, the seat of life, when animals are killed for food or for sacrificial purposes (Gen 9:2-4; Lev 17:10-14). Its stipulations also prohibit the taking of human life, which was created in God's own image (Gen 9:5-6; cf. 1:26-27). While the

---

27. The Priest emphasizes this connection between Noah and Sinai further by dating both Noah's first sighting of the earth after the flood (Gen 8:13) and the dedication of the tabernacle (Exod 40:2) to the first day of the Priestly liturgical year.

28. Sarna, *Genesis*, 60: "The destruction of the old world calls for the repopulation of the earth and the remedying of the ills that brought on the flood. Society must henceforth rest on more secure moral foundations. New norms of human behavior must be instituted."

covenant at Sinai will lay out the complete priestly legislation for Israel's religious life, and while the covenant with Abraham introduces the Israelite requirement of circumcision even before Sinai, the covenant with Noah introduces the world's first priestly legislation, which begins the new era of righteousness and provides the world's moral stability.

For the Priest, just as for the Storyteller, Noah founded the world's righteous age. And Noah founded this age for all his descendants. Thus, all the world's lineages shared Noah's righteousness and with it the stability that God's covenant with Noah brought to the world. Neither the Storyteller nor the Priest distinguish their own ethnicity from others on the basis of righteousness and sin. As we will see in the next chapter, the ancestors of other peoples often act more righteously than the members of Israel's own lineage. The Storyteller and the Priest do refer to Abraham and to Israel's other ancestors as righteous. But in doing so, they do not privilege them in any way as more righteous than others. By choosing the righteous Noah as their founding ancestor, they participate with all Noah's other descendants, that is, with all others in the world, in the righteous and stable world Noah founded.

Very early in the interpretation of Genesis, many interpreters began to supplement the Genesis narratives by attributing evil deeds, where none exist in the biblical text, to the generations between Noah and Abraham. As early as the creative reader who composed *Jubilees*, all kinds of new sins were attributed to humanity in the time before Abraham. According to *Jubilees*, Noah's sons made war on each other, captured cities, and sold slaves; Nimrod hunted down people and schemed to kill Abraham; Pathrusim and Casluhim snatched each other's wives; the princes of Shinar trampled on Torah; and Abraham's father and brothers made and worshipped idols in Ur, to name just a few examples.[29] Early interpreters also provided the first negative readings of the stories

---

29. *Jubilees* 10:27–12:8; the Deuteronomist also already attributes idolatry to Israel's distant ancestors in Mesopotamia (Josh 24:2), a view held by neither the Storyteller nor the Priest.

of Noah's vineyard and Babel.[30] Here is *Jubilees'* summary of the people who lived between Noah and Abraham: "After the flood they began... to grow old quickly and to shorten the days of their lives due to much suffering and due to the evil of their ways—except Abraham" (23:9).

Thereafter a host of Genesis's interpreters, from *Jubilees* onward, have supplied non-biblical evidence to make the claim that Abraham was Israel's first righteous ancestor, dividing an era of sin before him from an era of righteousness following him. None of these claims of evil deeds between Noah and Abraham are part of the Storyteller's or the Priest's narratives. They are additions to the biblical story. They do not in any way undermine the Storyteller's and the Priest's firm claim that Noah was their founding ancestor and the founder of a righteous world, and their belief that all shared in the righteousness and stability of this world.

Noah Founds a World of Blessing

Closely connected with Genesis's interpreters' view that Abraham begins the age of righteousness is their view that Abraham ushers in the age of blessing. To divide history at Abraham and present him as Israel's founding ancestor, these interpreters have characterized Genesis 1–11 before Abraham as an age under God's curse, and they have described the age of Israel's ancestors in Genesis 12–50, beginning with the blessing of Abraham in Genesis 12:1-3, as the age of God's blessing. In this traditional reading of Genesis, Abraham is history's turning point, the figure who reverses the world's curse and introduces blessing to his descendants and the members of his family.[31] In this way too, just as

---

30. See, for example, *Jubilees* 11:1-8, 14-17; 12:12-14; 21:21; 22:16; 23:9-10; *Genesis Rabbah* 37:2-5; 38:12-13.

31. Again, for some illustrative statements of this widespread view, see Norman Habel, *Literary Criticism of the Old Testament* (Philadelphia: Fortress, 1971), 52; and Levenson, *Inheriting Abraham*, 19, 20.

by their presentation of Abraham and his descendants as uniquely righteous, Genesis's interpreters have distinguished Israel from humanity in a way its authors never intended to do.

When we reexamine the themes of curse and blessing in Genesis, as we have the themes of sin and righteousness, we discover that here too Genesis's authors make Noah rather than Abraham the pivotal figure in their early history. Let's begin again with the Storyteller, who does indeed characterize the first age of his ancestral history as an age of curse—a curse, specifically, on the soil. In this age, God punishes wrongdoing by cursing the soil to block its fertility and its productivity (3:17; 4:11; 5:29; 8:21). When the first couple disobeys, God curses the farmer's arable soil with thorns and thistles (3:17-19). When Cain sins, God makes the soil completely unproductive for him (4:10-14). When the flood generation sins, God devastates all arable land, its farmers, and their livestock (6:5-7; cf. 5:29). This chilling drama of human sin and the soil's curse gives expression to the deepest fear of a subsistence agricultural society like Israel's: the failure of fallible farmers to survive on the land in a moral universe.[32]

In the Storyteller's narrative, Noah, not Abraham, reverses this primeval curse and ushers in the age of blessing. Noah, the flood hero, is born to free the people in the new age from the soil's curse (5:29). When Noah constructs the first altar and presents the first offering in the new age (8:20), God promises never again to curse the soil as punishment for its farmers' sins, and God guarantees stable agricultural seasons together with their harvests for all time (8:21-22). Immediately, Noah reestablishes agriculture by planting a vineyard (9:20). The Storyteller never again mentions the curse on the soil. Noah has brought the curse in history's first age to an end.

In the second age of history following the flood, the Storyteller introduces blessing for the first time. In this post-flood age, the Storyteller connects blessing with the flourishing of ethnic

---

32. Hiebert, *The Yahwist's Landscape*, 30–82, esp. 68–70.

identity and cultural well-being: blessing includes land, population, wealth, security, and status of a people or nation. For the Storyteller, blessing begins not with Abraham but with Noah, when he pronounces the first blessing of the new age: "Bless the LORD, the God of Shem" (9:26). When the Storyteller describes the renewal of this blessing to Abraham, he refers to the cultural well-being of the Israelite lineage to descend from him (12:2-3; 18:18; 22:17-18; 24:1, 35). Blessing plays the same role when it reappears with Isaac (26:3, 12, 24, 29) and Jacob (27:4, 25, 27-29, 30, 33; 30:30; 32:27, 30), and when Jacob passes it on to his sons, the forefathers of the people of Israel (49:28).

The Storyteller focuses in a particular and detailed way on the blessing received by Noah's descendants who are the ancestors of his own lineage: Shem, Abraham, Isaac, Jacob, and Jacob's sons. At the same time, he does not limit blessing to this lineage alone or distinguish his own ethnic group as the only participants in God's blessing. When we look at the Storyteller's view of non-Israelite lineages descended from Noah, we notice that he regards these lineages as blessed as well. He describes all the families and nations of the earth as blessed (12:3; 18:18; 22:18). How we are to understand the blessing of non-Israelite lineages in the post-flood era in relation to the blessing of Israel's own lineage has been debated extensively. If we understand the verb "bless" as passive, "be blessed," which is possible, it means that the blessings of those in Israel's lineage flow outward from them to benefit others, so that these others also share in the blessings of Israel's own lineage. Thus we would translate the blessing to Abraham and all others as "all the families of the earth will be blessed because of you" (12:3; cf. 28:14). If we understand the verb "bless" as reflexive, "bless themselves," which is also possible, it means that non-Israelite lineages will take as their own standard of blessing the blessings present among Israelite lineages. Thus, we would translate the blessing to Abraham and to others as "all the families of the earth will bless themselves by your blessing" (12:3). That is, may we be blessed as much as Abraham and his descendants are.[33] However we under-stand this verb, the Storyteller views the post-flood age as an age of widespread blessing. Israelite and non-Israelite lineages alike experience the broad ethnic and cultural well-being that the Sto-ryteller thinks of as blessing. The single exception is the curse on Canaan, a completely unique event to which we will return in the next chapter.[34]

The Priest, unlike the Storyteller, never mentions the curse. The Priest talks only about blessing in Israel's early history, and he focuses blessing on bearing children.[35] Like the Storyteller, the Priest in his own way uses the theme of blessing to divide history with the figure of Noah. He does so by adopting a pattern found in the Sumerian King List, where kingship is lowered from heaven at creation and lowered a second time after the flood to begin history's second age. In the Priest's version of Israel's early history, God blesses the first humans at creation by telling them to be fertile, multiply, and fill the earth (1:28; cf. 5:2). After destroy-ing the world with the flood, God reinstates the same blessing to Noah and his family (9:1, 7; cf. 8:17). The Priest makes Noah and his family, rather than Abraham and his family, the first to receive God's blessing in the new age, thereby extending this blessing to all Noah's descendants. The blessing of fertility is reiterated by the Priest in the post-flood era both to members of Israel's own lineage—Abraham (17:6), Isaac (25:11), and Jacob (35:9-11)—and to members of non-Israelite lineages, in particular Ishmael (17:20).

---

33. This debate has been complicated in the history of interpretation by Christian ex-egetes who have claimed the passive form in order to argue for the supercessionist passing of the blessing from Jews to Christians through Christ. See, for example, Jeffrey S. Siker, *Disin-heriting the Jews: Abraham in Early Christian Controversy* (Louisville: Westminster John Knox, 1991), and Jon Levenson, *Inheriting Abraham*.

34. The Storyteller's two references to curse in a hypothetical context (Gen 12:3; 27:29) simply promise the same curse as Canaan's for others who, like the Canaanites, might threaten Israel's security.

35. God also blesses the birds and sea creatures with fertility (Gen 1:22), and God blesses the Sabbath (2:3).

Just as all the members of Noah's family tree, those who are members of Israel's particular lineage and those who are not, share in Noah's righteousness, so all the members of Noah's family tree, those who are members of Israel's particular lineage and those who are not, share in Noah's blessing. Israel's earliest ancestors before the flood sinned and experienced the curse of the soil. But after the flood, all the descendants of Noah experience the righteousness and blessing that he introduced into the world. By choosing Noah as their founding ancestor, the Storyteller and the Priest choose all Noah's descendants as their family. By doing so, they place themselves inside the family of humanity and share with each of the other ethnic lineages the real world of history's second age, its righteousness, its blessings, and its covenant stability.

Noah's Family, Identity, and Difference

Abraham remains a powerful figure in three great Western religions. He continues to be an anchor for the formation of identity and a path toward communication across differences in Judaism, Christianity, and Islam. All three religions ground their identities, each in their various and distinctive ways, in Abraham. And all find in their common ancestry in his family an opportunity for relationship and communication between them. At the same time, Abraham has often also been used by Genesis's interpreters through history in an excessively exclusionary way to isolate one of the world's ethnicities, the descendants of Abraham, from others and to distinguish their ethnic identity in ways that the biblical text and its authors never intended. The Storyteller and the Priest, by recognizing Noah as their founding ancestor, held a more inclusive sense of their own genealogical identity and did not intend to shape their identity by granting their lineage more historical authenticity, truer righteousness, or greater blessing than the rest of humanity.

This exclusivist tendency is real and troubling because many of Genesis's interpreters isolate Israel from its world and choose to portray others in increasingly negative terms. James Kugel recognizes this tendency among the Bible's most ancient interpreters. Noting the polarized division of humanity into righteous and wicked in wisdom literature, Kugel observes "that a similar polarization takes place in ancient exegesis: biblical heroes are altogether good, with any fault air-brushed away, whereas figures like Esau or Balaam are altogether demonized—as if their neither-good-nor-evil status in the Bible itself was somehow intolerable."[36] We can recall here how the early interpreters of Genesis, like the author of *Jubilees*, add more and more lurid examples of sins committed by all the descendants of Noah after the flood, except Abraham and his lineage. We should ask ourselves how much we have been influenced by such exclusivist and negative interpretations of biblical texts. We recognize the fear of difference that lies in these interpretations of Genesis that, against the intention of its authors, isolates Israel's own ethnic identity from others and gives it a specially righteous status that was never claimed by the biblical text itself.

Recovering the more inclusivist identity constructed for their culture by the Storyteller and the Priest is a powerful antidote to such exclusivist ways of interpreting the Bible and thinking about difference today. And starting history with Noah is a powerful beginning in such more inclusivist thinking. In fact, within early Judaism, Noah played such an inclusive role. Early rabbinic debates about the salvation of Gentiles, that is, the role of non-Jews in the world to come, reveal both exclusivist and inclusivist views. This debate between Rabbi Eliezer and Rabbi Joshua b. Hananiah illustrates:

36. Kugel, *The Bible as It Was*, 27.

Rabbi Eliezer said: "All the nations will have no share in the world to come, even as it is said, 'The wicked shall go into Sheol, and all the nations that forget God.' (Ps. 9:17)...Rabbi Joshua said to him, "If the verse had said, 'The wicked shall go into Sheol with all the nations,' and had stopped there, I should have agreed with you, but as it goes on to say, 'who forget God,' it means that there are righteous men among the nations who have a share in the world to come."[37]

The inclusivist view of Rabbi Joshua eventually became the consensus in rabbinic Judaism. And when the rabbis set about determining the standards of righteousness required of Gentiles to participate in the world to come, they turned to Noah and to God's covenant with him. They found in Noah the figure who defined righteousness for all. "The rabbis linked the salvation of the Gentiles explicitly to the covenant made with Noah, and sealed with the rainbow," writes Alan Segal, "for in this covenant God promised mercy and deliverance to all mankind. The rabbis theorized that God gave all humanity 'natural' laws at that moment, the so-called Noahide Commandments, so that the whole human race could comprehend the meaning of righteousness."[38] Throughout the history of rabbinic Judaism, Noah and these Noahide Commandments have played this inclusive role, inviting all—members of the Jewish culture itself together with all others—into the world to come. The inclusivist consensus of rabbinic Judaism about identity and difference has, in its own powerful way, kept alive the viewpoint of the Storyteller and Priest described in this chapter.

Noah is thus a powerful image for understanding the *relationship* between identity and difference, between a single ethnicity like the people of Israel, to whom the Storyteller and the Priest belong, and all the other distinctive cultures of their world, the diverse world God brought about at Babel. The Storyteller and the

---

37. Alan F. Segal, *Rebecca's Children: Judaism and Christianity in the Roman World* (Cambridge, MA: Harvard University Press, 1986), 167.

38. Segal, *Rebecca's Children*, 170.

Priest articulate this relationship between their own ethnic identity and the different identities of their world is by the use of the language of family. By describing themselves as members of Noah's family, Genesis's authors claimed a familial relationship with all Noah's descendants, with all the different lineages and their identities descended from him. So the fundamental structure in the world underlying all its differences is the structure of relatedness. According to this way of thinking about difference, difference is real but always related in some way to one's own identity. Difference is always perceived within an underlying sense of relationship. The first fact about those with different identities is that they are relatives. This is a profoundly different way of thinking than starting with the notion of difference as the absence of relationship or connection.

This way of thinking about difference as grounded in familial relatedness is deeply present in the words of Sarsour, with which we began this chapter, where she describes her incredibly diverse neighborhood in Brooklyn as "a place where families and neighbors were one in the same," a place where "you did for your neighbor just as you would for an immediate family member." She calls her neighborhood "a community of radical love" and claims this experience of relationship in diversity as "the radical love that has powered me through my decades of work.... If I hadn't grown up believing that my neighbors are my family," she says, "I may not have cared, but it was in my nature to care about all these groups of people."[39] Her work on bringing together Muslim-Americans with other fearful Americans after 9/11 and her work bringing women of all persuasions together in the Women's March illustrates the power of her sense of relationship in diversity.

Identity and difference. The Storyteller and the Priest have again given us new lenses for thinking about ourselves and about others. By making Noah their founding ancestor, they affirmed in the strongest possible way the depth and legitimacy of their

---

39. Sarsour, "Linda Sarsour," 283, 292.

own ethnic identity as members of a small marginal kingdom in ancient West Asia. And at the same time, they affirmed in the strongest possible way that they were an integral part of a larger world in which difference was grounded in relatedness. They pass along to us lenses with great potential for rethinking the relationship between ourselves and others today.

Biblical Peoples Live with Difference

"How much space can we make for each other in our community, in our legacy, in our futures? Do we make enough space for the people who are different than us?"

—Tarell Alvin McCraney, author of *Choir Boy* and co-writer of *Moonlight*, in an interview with Jeffrey Brown on PBS NewsHour, February 22, 2019, 6:25 p.m. EDT

W hen I was translating the book of Genesis for the Common English Bible translation, I had the opportunity to read its great stories again very closely. They are stories of intrigue and deception, of conflict and disaster, and of rescue and redemption. I must confess, however, that in spite of their dramatic heights and depths, these stories were so familiar to me that reading them once again closely to translate them didn't really move me emotionally. I sensed once again their importance, but I knew them too well. I wasn't deeply touched by them. There was, however, one exception. That was the moment when Hagar, without water, desperate, weeping, having given up all hope, lays her son under a desert shrub and steps away. She can't bear to watch him die (Gen 21:15-16). No parent, no listener, can remain unmoved by such an experience. I wasn't, and I had to pause for a moment.

As I once again read the story of Sarah and Hagar and of Isaac and Ishmael to explore its significance for Israel's construction of its own identity, its view of others, and its thinking about living with difference, I realized that the story that had touched my humanity most deeply was a story one of Israel's authors had written about others. It revealed an imagination that could pull the listener into the life not just of his own people but into the lives of other people. It revealed an imagination that saw others with genuine humanity, that could enter their experience, that could feel their pain, and that could hope for their survival and their future. It revealed an imagination that had thought deeply about difference. It revealed an imagination that sought to express what living with difference could be like. It is this imagination that we will explore in this chapter.

In the first two chapters, we looked in a fresh way at the attitudes toward identity and difference held by the authors who wrote Israel's earliest history. In these narratives about the beginning of difference, Genesis's authors recognize the importance of ethnic particularity and group solidarity. They also truly accept the reality of difference and describe ways to think about difference within a framework of kinship relatedness. In the story of Babel in chapter 1, the Storyteller describes the search for ethnic identity as a core human need. It is humanity's primal act after the flood. The Storyteller also views difference as the norm for life in this world, the norm that was God's decision and that God built into the world at the beginning. In the story of Noah's descendants in chapter 2, the Storyteller and the Priest both show a deep interest in understanding the relationship between Israel's own identity and the identities of others. Through the language of kinship, they connect Israel with those who are different from them by including them in a common family tree. They situate difference within a kinship framework of relatedness. They consider inclusion rather than exclusion to be the primary context for thinking about difference.

In this chapter, we look at the remainder of the book of Genesis, where we find narratives about the actual interaction among different cultures. And we will see that the Storyteller and the Priest, and now also the Northern Storyteller, tell these stories, as they have from the very beginning of the book of Genesis, with the language of family and kinship. They think in familial concepts and language because they are members of a kinship society in which family is the core of all social relationships. Kinship language frames every relationship, from the relationship between brothers in an Israelite family to the relationship between the descendants of these brothers who make up peoples and nations. Identity and difference are family matters.

All the stories in Genesis speak on two levels. The first is the family level. At this level, each character represents a member of a typical Israelite family, just like the ones in which the authors of Genesis grew up. The typical Israelite family is a joint family, called the "father's house," composed of the male head of the household, his primary and secondary wives, their children, and servants and residents who have become members of the family through "fictive" kinship relationships. The rivalries that emerge in these families, as we will see, are typically between wives and husbands, between wives, and ultimately between sons over status in the family. Each story reflects the actual social dynamics and cultural realities of a typical Israelite family.

These stories of Genesis also speak at a second level. This is the level of peoples or nations. The major characters in these stories represent not only individuals in a typical Mediterranean agricultural family. They also represent the peoples or nations made up of their descendants. So, for example, Jacob, renamed Israel, represents a single individual ancestor and at the same time the entire people of Israel who count themselves as his descendants (Gen 35:9-13). His brother Esau, also named Edom, represents a single ancestor and at the same time the entire people of Edom who count themselves as his descendants (25:23-25; "red" [Esau's complexion] and Edom derive from the same Hebrew root). The stories about Jacob and Esau, therefore, are stories about the actual relationship between brothers in a typical family, and they are also stories about the relations between the Israelites and the Edomites who are their respective descendants. In the last story in Genesis, the story of Joseph and his brothers, each brother represents the tribal group descended from him, groups that make up the people of Israel itself. So this story is about the different groups within Israel's own ethnic identity.

In fact, for the authors of Genesis, this level of the stories, the level that speaks to the relationship between the peoples or the nations descended from their ancestors, may be the most important level. In this level of the story, Genesis's authors describe the realities of difference in their own world. They explain the relationships in their own later social and international context between their identity as Israelites and the different identities of their neighbors. By doing so, they convey to their listeners their values about the nature and importance of their own identity and also about their proper engagement with the different cultural identities among whom they live. We are especially interested in the way Genesis's authors articulate the relations between different cultures or peoples and the relations between the different tribal cultures that combine to shape their own ethnicity identity. Above all, we are interested in the values about identity and difference that these narratives reveal to us.

Four Great Family Stories

To grasp how Israel interacted with difference in its diverse world, how it constructed its own identity in that world, and how it viewed others with different identities, we will look at four great family narratives in Genesis. We will begin with the story of the first man, his wife, Eve, and their sons, Cain and Abel

(Gen 4:1-16), because this family narrative sets the context for the other stories of difference that follow in the book of Genesis. The three other family narratives, describing three successive generations, make up most of the book of Genesis: the story of Abraham, Sarah, and Hagar, and their sons, Isaac and Ishmael (Gen 12–13, 15–18, 20–23, 25); the story of Isaac, Rebekah, and their sons, Jacob and Esau (Gen 24–28, 32–33, 36); and the story of Jacob, Leah, Rachel, Zilpah, and Bilhah, and their twelve sons (Gen 29–31, 34–35, 37–50). The first two of these narrative cycles have an "international" character. In the first of these, Genesis's authors explore their relationship to their neighbors the Ishmaelites, Ishmael's descendants, and in the second of these they define their relationship to the Edomite people, Esau's (Edom's) descendants. The third narrative cycle about Jacob's twelve sons, who are the ancestors of Israel's twelve tribes, is "national" in character. It explains and legitimates the relationship among the tribal groups that comprise the people of Israel itself. In this story, we will examine living with difference within an ethnic community.

These four great family stories are designed to explore the interaction between cultures and their negotiation of difference. They are fashioned to address a single question: When tensions arise because of differences between individuals or groups, how should the parties respond to their differences and forge a future? Each narrative follows the same plot line. First, a conflict arises and develops. The rivalry between different parties that will drive the story's action flares up and builds. Second, the competing characters respond immediately with harmful intent and deadly force. They threaten each other's very existence and act to destroy their relationship. Finally, the stories seek to find a path toward survival and the means to construct a future in which both parties can thrive. These narratives do not present simple conflicts, responses, and resolutions. They are complicated and textured.

The three-part structure of these stories reveals the most fundamental views about living with difference held by Genesis's authors. By beginning with conflict in every story, Genesis's authors show how realistic and unsentimental they are about the challenges of difference. They talk about conflict because they have a deep sense of the fragility of social relationships, from the most intimate ones in families to the largest ones in international relations. They know from experience how differences, from the personal level of brothers to the broad level of peoples, can create tensions, competition, rivalries, threats, and violence, and can ultimately cause the breakdown of relationships and communities. By describing the harmful intent and deadly actions in response to these tensions, Genesis's authors show us how deeply they understand both the vulnerability and the importance of social networks, whether within families or international communities. They recognize the high stakes of difference. They know that community is essential for life, and they know how quickly it can break down. They begin their exploration of difference by facing the real world and its divisions squarely without flinching.

Though absolutely realistic about the challenges of difference, Genesis's authors are not pessimists. They are ultimately optimistic about living with difference in families that face conflicts and about living in a world defined by its diverse cultures. They tell stories that find ways forward through conflicts, which describe imaginative and courageous ways to respond to threats, and in which individuals and groups construct a world where differences can grow and flourish, a world where ethnic identities are not subsumed or destroyed but recognized and respected. Throughout Genesis, its authors are, of course, telling *their* story, the story of their people, known as Israel. In this sense, Israel's writers embrace the core human experience of membership in a particular ethnic community. And we will see that they claim for themselves a particular identity, power, and status in their world that is unique to themselves.

At the same time, Genesis's authors are profoundly interested in others, in others' identities, and in Israel's relationships to them. First, they place a premium on the relationships underlying their differences. They do this by the use of kinship language, by which they establish their relationship to others as members of the same family. They resolve conflict in each of these stories, except the first, by reconstructing kinship relationships that are threatened with extinction. Second, Genesis's authors respect others as occupying a place in the world as legitimate as their own, thereby recognizing fully the multiple and distinct ethnicities among which they live. They consider difference normal. Third, they grant others full humanity within their human family. They tell stories about them that draw the listener sympathetically into their neighbor's experiences. Finally, Genesis's authors view all peoples under the care of the God they know, and they believe that all peoples share equally in the world of righteousness and blessing their founding ancestor Noah brought about. They even recognize moments when their neighbors act with such generosity and compassion that they themselves prosper from others' acts of kindness toward them. In all these ways, the great family stories in Genesis provide lessons for their first listeners about living with difference, just as they may for us today.

The book of Genesis actually contains more encounters between Israel and others than we will be able to explore in these four great family narratives that make up the majority of the book. In addition to these stories about Israel and the Ishmaelites and Edomites, and of the tribes within Israel itself, other narratives explore Israel's relationship to the Egyptians (Gen 12:10-20), the Moabites and Ammonites (19:29-38), the Philistines (20:1-18; 21:22-34; 26:1-32), the Arameans (31:43-55), and the Shechemites (34:1-31), to name the major examples. These encounters are important to understand fully Israel's view of itself and others in the book of Genesis, but we will not have space to deal with them here. I can say confidently, however, that the portrayal of identity and difference that we see developed in the four great family stories comprehensively represents the portrayal of identity and difference in these other encounters as well.

Cain and Abel (Genesis 4:1-16)

We continue our exploration of identity and difference with the story of the first family in Genesis, the story of Cain and Abel, because it represents the negative archetype for all that follows. It describes the complete failure to engage conflict constructively and to negotiate difference. It describes the absolute breakdown of relationship. This story refuses to flinch from what can happen. By doing so, it provides a weighty and cautionary tale as the backdrop for the three great post-flood family stories in the book of Genesis, stories that all move through conflict and honor difference. The story of Cain and Abel is from the hand of the Storyteller, who is also the primary architect of the great family stories to follow. It follows the plot that drives each of these stories, from conflict through threat toward resolution.

The story of the first family in Genesis, like the stories to follow, describes life in a typical Israelite family. The family lives on a typical Israelite subsistence farm, with the first son, Cain, who receives the primary share of the family's land, taking up farming, and the second son, Abel, as later sons typically did, taking care of the family's flocks (Gen 4:2).[1] In the stories after the flood, conflict arises between sons seeking favored status in the family and their father's favor and primary blessing. In this story, however, God alone introduces the conflict by looking favorably on Abel's offering and unfavorably on Cain's (4:3-5). Interpreters have spent most of their time and energy explaining and justifying God's preference for Abel's sacrifice. All their explanations are theories that go beyond the story and lack definitive evidence, and most

---

1. Theodore Hiebert, *The Yahwist's Landscape: Nature and Religion in Early Israel* (New York: Oxford University Press, 1996), 38–41.

are directed toward finding some flaw in Cain to explain God's lack of approval and justify God's decision. However, the Storyteller, remarkably, refuses to explain God's decision. We must take him seriously and recognize that he didn't intend to explain God's decision. His intention was to explore how the sons of the world's first family would deal with their conflict and with their differences. That's why he's built his entire story around the dramatic conflict between the brothers and how it will be handled.

In this story, just as in the family stories to follow, the Storyteller refuses to describe conflict in simplistic terms. The listener sympathizes with Cain, the family's oldest child, who is born into a position of unique status as the family's primary heir, who offers God the produce from farming the family's land, and who, without explanation, is suddenly disfavored. Since the Storyteller provides no other facts from which to judge, Cain's resentment and anger are understandable. We would feel that way too. But as Cain contemplates revenge, the listener fears for his brother Abel. So when Cain invites Abel out into the field, the listener's fear becomes palpable. The listener's sympathy with Abel, who is now completely vulnerable, becomes nearly absolute.

Cain responds to conflict with violence. He responds to difference by eliminating it. This is the threat that hangs in the air during Cain's and God's conversations at the center of the story (4:5-10). "The LORD said to Cain, 'Why are you angry and why do you look so resentful? If you do the right thing, won't you be accepted? But if you don't do the right thing, sin will be waiting at the door ready to strike. It will entice you, but you must rule over it" (4:6-7). God offers Cain a choice: "Overcome your anger and resentment, find a way through your disappointment, choose a future in which both of you can live, and you will be accepted. Give in to your anger, kill your brother, and the evil at your door will engulf both of you." Cain chooses to end the relationship and to eliminate his brother. His story ends without resolution. It ends in death.

This story takes place in the age before the flood. Thereby, it plays a distinctive role among all these stories. First, it speaks only to the family level, not to the level of peoples and nations, which, as we've seen in chapter 2, only emerge in the age after the flood. Second, as we've also seen in chapter 2, this story takes place in the old age before the flood, the old age of Israel's ancestral sinners and the soil's curse, the old age of Israel's previous identity that no longer defines it. Noah, Israel's righteous founding ancestor, brings this age to an end and provides Israel, together with Noah's other descendants, an entirely new identity of righteousness and blessing.

The story of Cain killing his brother Abel in the age before the flood is meant by the Storyteller to be the negative archetype of the relation between people (or peoples) for all time to come. It's a reflection of Israel's old identity. In Cain's act, the other is eliminated, erased. The relationship between people is destroyed. God counsels Cain against such an irreparable response to another, in this case, to his own brother (4:6). In the stories of sibling rivalry after the flood, the new post-flood age that is introduced by Israel's founding ancestor Noah, the erasure of the other never happens again. Rivalries are always negotiated and resolved in the interest of the welfare of all parties, and they are most often resolved by the compassion of the most wronged and the most powerful individual. When another is erased in Noah's age after the flood, as when Jacob's sons Simeon and Levi kill the Shechemites for what the sons perceive as a violation, Jacob rebukes them and removes them from the line of succession in his family (34:1-31; 49:5-7).

Yet, though he is the Storyteller's archetypal antihero, Cain himself is never abandoned by the Storyteller, nor is he placed beyond the pale of God's care. Cain remains the central character in the Storyteller's drama. According to the Storyteller, Cain forever lives under God's protection and safety when God marks him to keep him safe (4:15). While exiled from his family and its land, he is not cast aside by God in spite of his terrible past (4:13-15).

In fact, the Storyteller makes Cain the ancestor of all to come, the ancestor of Noah himself, Israel's own founding ancestor (4:17-24; 5:29). By contrast, the Priest, too troubled by Cain's act, removes Cain from Israel's ancestry, replacing him with his brother Seth (5:1-6). Even the Storyteller's archetypal antihero, the one who violently erases the other, never himself is erased.

Isaac and Ishmael/Israelites and Ishmaelites (Genesis 12–13, 15–18, 20–23, 25)

The story of Abraham, his wives, Sarah and Hagar, and their sons, Isaac and Ishmael, is the first of the three great post-flood stories. It describes the lineage (Sarah and Isaac) from which the Israelites originate as well as the lineage (Hagar and Ishmael) from which their neighbors the Ishmaelites originate. So, it is not just the story of a single Israelite family, like the pre-flood story of Cain and Abel. It is a story that speaks to two levels, the level of the family, but also, and most importantly for us, the level of the peoples descended from the members of this family. It reveals the way in which Genesis's authors articulate their own identity as Israelites through the lineage of Sarah and Isaac, and it also reveals how Genesis's authors view the Ishmaelites through the narratives of the lineage of Hagar and Ishmael. The story reveals the nature of the relationship between the Israelites and the Ishmaelites, and between the descendants of Isaac and Ishmael, as the authors of Genesis viewed this relationship in their own time. All three of Genesis's authors, the Storyteller, the Northern Storyteller, and the Priest, preserve traditions about Isaac and Ishmael.

The conflict that begins the story of Isaac (and his descendants the Israelites) and Ishmael (and his descendants the Ishmaelites) arises in the same way it will in all the post-flood stories. It springs from a competition for the position as the family's primary heir and for the status, privilege, power, and resources the primary heir receives. The Priest preserves no traditions about the origin of the conflict itself. But the Storyteller (Gen 16:1-14) and the Northern Storyteller (21:8-21) both provide dramatic accounts of it. In both of their versions, Isaac's and Ishmael's mothers are deeply involved. Each woman wishes to see her own son promoted, and each is also looking out for herself, since her own status in the family is tied to her son's status. In the Storyteller's account, Sarah feels disrespected by Hagar after Hagar becomes pregnant with Ishmael, and she feels her position as primary wife is threatened. She treats Hagar so badly that the pregnant Hagar decides to flee from Abraham's household (16:4-6, 8). In the Northern Storyteller's version, Sarah is upset that Ishmael might share the family inheritance with her son Isaac, and she forces Abraham to send Ishmael and Hagar away to ensure that Isaac alone will inherit the family's wealth (21:8-10).

Both of the Storytellers have shaped their dramas of rivalry between two sons and their mothers, not to denounce it but to recognize reality and to invite the listener into both sides of the conflict. On the one hand, we sympathize with Sarah, whose legitimate status as primary wife is threatened, and her husband Abraham does nothing to protect her and her place in the family. On the other hand, we sympathize with Hagar, whose pregnancy is just what Sarah and Abraham had asked of her and whose place in the household is put in jeopardy when Sarah defends her own place in the family. We are especially distressed when Hagar is forced out of Abraham's household and when her and her son's lives are placed in jeopardy.

In these accounts of conflict, the offended party, Israel's ancestor, responds not to annihilate the other, as Cain did, but to distance the other. However, this distancing of the other is so severe and so dangerous that the threat of death of the other becomes a real possibility. Hagar and her son nearly die in the desert. However, this story, unlike the story of Cain and Abel, finds a way forward. It plots a future in which both parties of the conflict survive, grow, and flourish. It builds a world in which ethnic identities are not subsumed or destroyed but recognized and respected. It tells of a world in which cultural identity and cultural difference can thrive. And it attributes that world and that future of both peoples to God. In both the Storyteller's and the Northern Storyteller's versions of the conflict, the same God who ensures that Isaac will be Abraham's heir intervenes to protect Ishmael and to give his mother, Hagar, the same promises of descendants and nationhood given to Abraham and Isaac. God acts to make both peoples thrive.

In the story of Isaac and Ishmael, Genesis's three authors each traces his own identity as an Israelite through Sarah and Isaac. In so doing, they ascribe to Israel a distinctive status in several ways. First, they present their own lineage as descended from Sarah, Abraham's primary wife. By contrast, Ishmael's lineage descends from Hagar, Sarah's servant and Abraham's secondary wife (16:1-3). At the same time, we must not forget that all Genesis's authors recognized Ishmael as Abraham's firstborn son. Second, the Priest states that God's covenant relationship with Abraham will be continued through Isaac and through his descendants, not through Ishmael and his descendants (17:2, 19-21). Finally, and this distancing is the element of the story that attracts everyone's central attention, Ishmael and Hagar are forced to leave Abraham's household, so that Isaac will flourish there as Abraham's primary heir.

We might expect that Genesis's authors intended these claims for Isaac's primary status and these stories of the banishment of Ishmael and his non-Israelite lineage to separate and isolate the Ishmaelites as strongly as possible from the Israelites, their relationship to God, and their own well-being. But by focusing on Ishmael's expulsion alone without examining the story more closely, we overlook the powerful ways Genesis's authors shape their stories of Ishmael to claim their own close relationship to the Ishmaelites, to acknowledge the Ishmaelites' relationship to God and their place in God's world, and to recognize the Ishmaelites' special status among their neighbors.

Genesis's authors claim an extraordinarily close relationship to the Ishmaelites. They do this through the language of family, kinship, and genealogy that, as we have seen, governs all their understandings of their relationships with others. As the son of Abraham, and brother of Israel's father, Isaac, Ishmael is quite literally Israel's uncle, to place their relationship within the family Israel claims for itself. The relationship between Israelites and Ishmaelites is, therefore, closer than any other of their neighbors, except for the Edomites, who originate in the next generation as the descendants of Israel's own brother, Esau (Edom). While we might consider Ishmael's departure from Abraham's household to distance him entirely from a relationship with Isaac, Genesis's authors have constructed a family tree to claim the Ishmaelites as the Israelites' second-closest relatives.

Together with this claim for their own close relationship to the Ishmaelites, Genesis's authors stress the Ishmaelites' relationship to God and their place in God's world, as well as the Ishmaelites' special status among their neighbors. To understand these claims most clearly, it is best to hear them from Genesis's individual authors themselves. Let's begin with the earliest writer, the Storyteller. The Storyteller conveys his view of God's relationship to the Ishmaelites by describing God's appearance to Hagar in the desert after she leaves Abraham's household (16:7-14). It is striking that the Storyteller preserves no account of God's appearance to Sarah, Abraham's primary wife, through whom the Storyteller traces his own lineage. He does preserve an account of God's direct appearance to Hagar, Sarah's servant and Abraham's secondary wife, through whom the Ishmaelites descend.

In God's encounter with Hagar, God notices Hagar's distress (16:9, 11), just as God notices the Israelites' distress at a later time when the Storyteller describes Israel's harsh treatment under slavery in Egypt (Exod 3:7-8). In fact, Ishmael's name means "God hears." Then God responds to Hagar's distress by promising her uncountable descendants (Gen 16:11), the same promise God makes to the ancestors in Israel's own lineage, to Abraham (13:16), to Isaac (26:3-4), and to Jacob (28:14). Finally, and remarkably, Hagar names God. Her name for God, El Roi, means that God has seen her and/or she has seen God. In all these ways, Hagar's encounter with God compares to or exceeds the encounter with God experienced by Israel's own ancestors.

The Northern Storyteller is equally respectful of the relationship between God and the Ishmaelites and of the Ishmaelites' status in the world (21:8-21). When in his account, Abraham protests Sarah's demand that Hagar and Ishmael be removed from his household, God assures Abraham that God will make Ishmael's descendants a great nation (21:13, 18), the same promise God made to Ishmael's father Abraham (12:2). Then, God intervenes to protect Ishmael in the desert: God hears Ishmael's cries of distress (21:17-18) and saves him and his mother from death by finding them water (21:19). The Northern Storyteller then tells us that "God remained with the boy," as he grew up and became an expert archer, a respected skill certainly connected by this Storyteller with Ishmael's descendants (21:20-21). In the view of the Northern Storyteller too, Ishmael's success and place in the world are ensured by God's protection and care.

In their accounts of Ishmael's departure from Abraham's household, both of these Storytellers reveal a clear discomfort about Ishmael's separation from Abraham's household through their sympathy with Hagar's and Ishmael's plight. The Storyteller communicates this by God's close attention to Hagar and to her pain and God's intention to protect her and make her descendants flourish (16:7-11). Though Sarah was within her prerogatives as the primary wife to demand subservience from Hagar, the Storyteller focuses his attention on Hagar, and our emotions are drawn toward her. The Northern Storyteller communicates his discomfort through his ancestor Abraham's own distress and pleas to God that Ishmael stay, and also through God's assurance to protect Hagar and her son (21:11-13). Like the Storyteller, the Northern Storyteller also focuses his narrative on Hagar's and Ishmael's plight, rather than on Sarah's prerogatives, and he raises deeper sympathies for Ishmael's future rather than for his own. These Storytellers display remarkable power to pull the listener not just into the lives of their own people but also into the lives of others. They reveal an imagination to see the humanity in others, to know them deeply, and to build relationships across differences.

One more point needs to be made about these stories of Ishmael's forced departure. They are strongly driven by both Storytellers' interest in explaining the Ishmaelites' connection to their land, one of the primary markers of ethnicity in Genesis. The Ishmaelites, as we know from their appearance elsewhere in Genesis, are camel traders, moving through the ancient West Asian desert fringes surrounding Israel (37:25, 28; 39:1). Accordingly, the Storyteller's account places Hagar in the southern desert when she receive God's announcement of Ishmael's birth (16:7-11). He also claims that a famous well in this desert, Beer-lahai-roi, is named for Hagar's encounter with God there (16:13-14). Further, he compares Ishmael to a tough desert animal, the wild mule, and describes the conflicts Ishmael's descendants will face because of distrust sedentary cultures often hold for nomadic traders (16:12). The Northern Storyteller too locates the Ishmaelites in the southern desert, placing Hagar and her son there (21:14) and describing Ishmael's growth into an accomplished desert archer (21:20-21). By connecting Ishmael's origins with the desert, both Storytellers account for key aspects of the Ishmaelites' ethnicity, their home in the desert, their trading economy, and their skills at archery.

Of Genesis's three authors, the Priest may be the Israelite writer who presents Ishmael and his lineage in the most positive and sympathetic light of all. The Priest, as we've already noted, preserves no traditions of his own of Ishmael's departure from Abraham's household. In the Priest's account of God's covenant with Abraham in Genesis 17, Abraham pleads with God to make Ishmael his primary heir, in spite of God's promise to Abraham that Sarah's son, Isaac, will continue the covenant line of Israel's lineage (17:15-19). In response to Abraham's plea for Ishmael, God promises to give Ishmael uncountable descendants and to make Ishmael's descendants a great nation made up of twelve tribal leaders (17:20), all promises made to Abraham and Israel's own lineage. Furthermore, while God specifically describes Isaac as the carrier of Abraham's covenant (17:19, 21), Ishmael actually participates in the Abrahamic covenant, the requirement of which is circumcision (17:9-14). On the day of God's covenant with Abraham, Ishmael, together with Abraham and all the men of Abraham's household, is circumcised (17:23-27). Finally, in what might be the most poignant detail about Ishmael in all these traditions, Ishmael and Isaac reunite to bury their father on the land he had purchased for his and Sarah's burial (25:7-10).

The Genesis stories of Isaac and Ishmael construct an image of the relationship between themselves and others in which rivalry does not end in annihilation, as it does in the archetypal negative story of Cain and Abel (though it comes close to annihilation when Hagar—out of water, desperate, and full of grief—sets her son down under a desert shrub to die). You could say that in the story of Isaac and Ishmael, rivalry is resolved by separation, not by annihilation. But this separation is neither Israel's effort to isolate another people nor a dismissal of them. After their separation, both peoples flourish, and they flourish because God intends that they both flourish. While they have clearly distinguished their own lineage from the lineage of the Ishmaelites, Genesis's authors have done so in a way that claims an extraordinarily close relationship with them, a respect for their unique and powerful place in the world, and the belief that their identity and their success is the result of God's intentions for them and for the world in which they live.

Jacob and Esau/Israelites and Edomites (Genesis 24–28, 32–33, 36)

In the story of Jacob and Esau, the Storyteller explores the negotiation of difference between his own people, the Israelites, and their nearest neighbors, the Edomites. The arc of the story of Jacob (Israel) and Esau (Edom) follows the same pattern of conflict, response, and resolution we've already seen in the stories of Cain and Abel and Isaac and Ishmael. The Storyteller is the primary architect of this family's story of conflict, response, and resolution. The Northern Storyteller preserves only traditions about the birth of Jacob's sons during his exile from his home (Gen 30:1-24a) and about Jacob's treaty with Laban the Aramean (31:43-48, 50-54) on his return. And the Priest provides minor editorial additions, together with one distinctive viewpoint we will discuss in a moment. But the drama we will describe here and the values about difference it reflects are essentially the Storyteller's.

The Storyteller identifies the source of the conflict between Jacob (Israel) and Esau (Edom)—just as of the conflict between Isaac and Ishmael—as a competition for the position as the family's primary heir and for the status, privilege, power, and resources the primary heir receives. According to Israelite law and custom, the oldest male laid claim to special status, authority over his brothers, and the major share of his father's possessions. We see this when Isaac blesses Jacob, Israel's ancestor (thinking he was blessing his firstborn Esau, Edom's ancestor), with agricultural bounty and makes him more powerful than his brothers (27:27-29, 37; cf. Deut 21:17). In this story, Esau, Edom's ancestor, rather than

Jacob, Israel's ancestor, is the oldest male with his related rights, rights he loses through Jacob's deception.

Isaac, the head of his household, holds the power to select his family's primary heir (Gen 27:1-4). Isaac selects Esau, Edom's ancestor, both because he was his oldest son and because he was his favorite son. "Isaac loved Esau, because he enjoyed eating game, but Rebekah loved Jacob" (25:28). Isaac admired Esau's hunting prowess and the delicious game he prepared (25:27-28; 27:1-4, 19, 32). By preferring Esau, Isaac resembles Abraham's preference for Ishmael, who was his oldest son but who did not become his primary heir (16:5; 17:18). Isaac's plan to make Esau his primary heir conforms to Israelite custom that was intended to ensure an orderly transition from one generation to the next and to keep the family intact, stable, and strong.

Conflict arises and the family is destabilized when Isaac's wife, Rebekah, decides to promote their second-born son and her favorite, Jacob, as Isaac's primary heir (25:27-28; 27:5-8). To achieve their aim, Rebekah and Jacob, who hold positions of secondary status and power in the family as wife and second-born son, subvert the customary rules of Israel's kinship society. We know the story. Rebekah dresses Jacob in Esau's clothes and cooks a meal for him to present to Isaac as though he were Esau (27:9-17). Isaac, old and blind, blesses Jacob, thinking he's making Esau his primary heir but giving this position to Jacob instead, a blessing that he can't withdraw (27:18-29, 33). Isaac and Esau are both horribly distressed, and Isaac can only provide Esau with a secondary blessing (27:30-40). Thus the most elemental conflict at the most intimate level of Israel's kinship society arises: the family's sons (with their parents' involvement) struggle over the position of primary heir and the special status, authority, and resources that this position carries.

The Storyteller shapes this drama of sibling rivalry, again, not to denounce it but to draw the listener sympathetically into both sides of the conflict. On the one hand, Esau's grief and ultimately murderous intent is hardly unexpected, given the future he deserves, expects, and loses (27:34, 41). The traditional structures of the Israelite family guarantee the primary status and authority of the patriarch and his oldest son. And they are taken from him, Esau himself says, by treachery and deceit (27:35-36). The only way to recover what was rightfully his was to eliminate the one who had stolen it from him and to reclaim his lawful and proper place.

On the other hand, Rebekah and Jacob chose the only path open to those who were born into disadvantaged positions in kinship society. To achieve status, they must subvert the patriarchal structures that reign in the biblical family. Subversion like this is not unique. It occurs in each of these stories when non-firstborn sons—Isaac and Jacob—become the family's primary heirs. It is part of the Storyteller's own experience. And to provide further sympathy for this challenge to traditional family structures, the conflict it involved, and the outcome it produced, the Storyteller, in his introductory episode to the Jacob and Esau stories, describes God appearing to Rebekah to announce that her older son would serve her younger son (25:21-26). Rebekah and Jacob, therefore, act out God's own promises.

Esau's anger is understandable. But acting upon it will destroy the family, just as Cain's action destroyed the first family before the flood. To save Jacob from Esau's murderous plans, Rebekah sends him away, and death is averted by temporary exile. Jacob flees and takes up residence with his relatives in Haran (27:41-45). In contrast to the Storyteller's explanation for Jacob's departure, the Priest interjects an entirely different motivation. Jacob must travel to find a wife among his maternal uncle's daughters. This would avert the prospect of marrying a Canaanite woman, someone outside of his kinship network (27:46–28:5). Such marriage outside of one's kinship community, a concern not shared by the Storyteller himself, became an issue during the exile and postexilic period of the Priest himself, when a small and decimated Judahite community struggled to keep its own identity intact in a social context where it was severely threatened. It appears that the Priest has embedded in his ancestral stories the concern of his own day about threats to identity that intermarriage posed. Yet even here, the Priest respects Esau enough to tell us that he took his parents' advice and married within the family (28:6-9).

The resolution of this story of conflict, the threat of death, and the anticipated end of the relationship between brothers and peoples hardly takes place in the way we might expect. At least not in a story told from Israel's own point of view. When the Storyteller resumes the narrative of Jacob and Esau, after Jacob's stay with his Aramean relatives, Esau, Edom's ancestor, becomes the hero of the story (Gen 32–33). He preserves the life of his brother Jacob, Israel's ancestor. Esau, who has reason to take revenge on Jacob and who has the power to do so, doesn't. He puts the conflict behind him entirely. He embraces his brother and reestablishes the relationship between them. The Storyteller's entire narrative of reconciliation leads up to Esau's act of humanity, generosity, and respect.

When Jacob (Israel's ancestor) returns home to face Esau (Edom's ancestor), Jacob is frightened, contrite, and subservient. He recognizes Esau's superior strength and his understandable reason for revenge (32:6-8). He knows he has taken Esau's rightful place in the family, he pleads for Esau's kindness (32:5; 33:8, 15), and he offers gifts to placate Esau's anger (32:7-8, 13-15, 20-21; 33:10-11). In spite of having been given authority over his brothers (25:23; 27:29), Jacob expresses complete subservience to Esau. He calls Esau his "master/lord," and refers to himself as Esau's "servant" (32:4, 5, 18, 20; 33:5, 8, 13, 14, 15). He and his family bow to Esau when they meet (33:3, 6-7). Esau recognizes Jacob as his brother. Surprisingly, against Jacob's expectations and our own, Esau runs to meet Jacob, throws his arms around him, kisses him, and weeps (33:3-4). He even offers Jacob assistance from his own wealth (33:12-15). Esau, Edom's ancestor, honors his kinship to his brother above the rivalry between them. He restores their relationship.

In this narrative of Israel and Edom, the Storyteller articulates the shape of his own ethnic identity by legitimating Israel's position as the primary heir in the lineage of Abraham and Isaac, holding its unique status, privilege, power, and resources. His Israelite identity included possession of the land that biblical Israel inhabited, along with its agricultural bounty (27:27-28). It also included power over his brothers, that is, over the descendants of his brothers, the Edomites, as Isaac explicitly states: "May the nations serve you, may peoples bow down to you" (27:29). The Storyteller's claims thus describe and legitimate Israel's actual military superiority in his own day, or, as is also possible, they may represent the desire for military superiority at a time when Israel did not possess it. Isaac's words in his blessing to Esau suggest a continuing rivalry between Israel and Edom over superior strength and hegemony in their area of influence (27:40).

The Storyteller legitimates this special status of his people Israel, however, in a complex and somewhat enigmatic way. Israel's status is only achieved by Jacob and Rebekah violating the kinship structures at the heart of community as the Storyteller knew it and by igniting a conflict that could have destroyed it. Some interpreters believe the Storyteller meant to make the theological point that God determines the future without regard to human conventions. However, the Storyteller's point is actually more nuanced. He recognizes the rigidity built into the patriarchal kinship structures of his society and regularly experiences the challenges brought against these structures by the "subordinate" members of such a society, in particular, wives and second sons. He wishes to explore the consequences of the conflict such challenges create and the possible paths toward resolution. How can societies and international communities forge a way forward when inevitable struggles for status and resources erupt? The fact that the Storyteller casts his own ancestor Jacob (Israel) as a challenge to convention may mean that he intended to legitimate King David himself, who was Jesse's seventh son. Even more important, it may mean that he recognizes the complex nature of conflict and does not want to oversimplify it by portraying it as merely a struggle between right and wrong. It is a struggle that arises from the imbalance of power within kinship itself.

By casting the ancestor of his neighboring Edomites as Isaac's oldest son, the Storyteller intends to grant them a privileged place among Israel's relationships in its political sphere. Indeed, the Storyteller views Esau, and thereby his descendants, the Edomites, with deep respect. He claims Edom as the closest member of his own kinship network: Jacob's twin brother and Isaac's firstborn son. He legitimates Edom's claim to their land, Seir, east of the Dead Sea, the name that is connected to Esau's own hairy complexion at his birth (25:25). Esau takes up residency there at the end of this narrative (33:16). And Isaac blesses Esau with agricultural bounty in his land just as he does Jacob in his own land, a blessing that has been turned into a curse of exile by many translators (Gen 27:39). The Hebrew preposition *min*, "from," can just as easily be translated "from" as "far away from." Rather than assigning him a home "far away from the olive groves of the earth" (CEB; NRSV, "away from"), Isaac grants Esau a home "from," or "from the resources of," the olive groves of the earth. Both Jacob and Esau inhabit their own lands and reap agricultural bounty from them.

Finally, and most remarkably, the Storyteller portrays Esau, the ancestor of the Edomites, as a man of genuine humanity, great strength, strong commitment to kinship bonds, and broad generosity. Esau (Edom) is the one who puts aside past wrongs and restores the kinship relationship that Jacob (Israel) by his deceit has placed in jeopardy. In spite of what he has lost to his brother, Esau embraces him with great warmth in the most emotional scene in the story (33:4). He is the firstborn. And he is the favorite of Israel's ancestor, Isaac (25:27; 27:1-2). He has been done a disservice by those interpreters who wish to "other" him by making him a rough and rustic fellow, too small-minded to avoid selling his birthright to Jacob for a bowl of lentils when he was hungry (25:27-34). This short episode is a tradition more intent on taking the blame off of Jacob for gaining the birthright unfairly than throwing aspersions on Esau. It in no way undermines the admirable image of Esau drawn by the Storyteller in the arc of his narrative. In the end, the Storyteller fashioned a narrative that at once describes and legitimates his own people's distinctive place in the world while, at the same time, does not disparage others or separate themselves from them. In fact, the Storyteller credits others, his brothers the Edomites in this case, with saving and restoring the relationship between the Israelites and their neighbors, the Edomites.

Joseph and His Brothers/ The Twelve Tribes of Israel (Genesis 29–31, 34–35, 37–50)

In the stories of Jacob's twelve sons that we consider next, Genesis's authors explore the negotiation of difference not between Israel and others but among the various communities that make up the people of Israel itself. So we are looking here at Israel's construction of its own identity. And we will see how much difference that ethnic identity incorporates within itself and how "multicultural" that identity really is. Again, the Storyteller is the primary architect of this drama, but the Northern Storyteller also makes significant contributions to the narrative and to Israel's definition of itself, which we will also acknowledge.

The larger level this family drama speaks to is the level of the tribes that comprise the people of Israel, each claiming descent from one of Jacob's twelve sons. Joseph, the main character of this drama, is a slight exception to this rule, since he is the father of two of Israel's tribal groups, the tribes of Ephraim and Manasseh (Gen 48:1-22). As we might expect, the account in Genesis 48 of the blessing of Joseph's sons and their incorporation into the tribes of Israel comes from the Northern Storyteller's traditions. Ephraim and Manasseh were the primary tribal communities in the north. The north was larger and wealthier than was Judah, which was David's tribe and home base. For David to unite the southern and northern tribes into a single kingdom, he had to approach and gain the loyalty of the northerners from Ephraim and Manasseh, Joseph's sons (2 Sam 5:1-5). In this drama, therefore, Joseph, the hero, represents the northern tribes of Ephraim and Manasseh, who held most of the land and wealth that became part of David's united kingdom.

Judah, the other hero of the story, is the ancestor of the tribe of Judah located in the south and the tribe into which David was born. As we've already noted, Judah became the name for the Southern Kingdom of Israel. In this drama of Jacob's twelve sons, the figure of Judah represents not just the tribe of Judah but also the figure of David, who was a member of that tribe. In a way, he also represents the great Davidic dynasty, which ruled from Jerusalem, and is certainly the home of the Storyteller himself. The Storyteller's account of Jacob's twelve sons, as we will see, explains the elevation of Judah to the primary position in Jacob's family and his role in uniting a diverse group of tribes and communities, including especially the northern tribes that descended from Joseph, into the single people of Israel.

This family drama, like those before it, begins in conflict. And its conflict is ignited by the same rivalry present in the generations that precede it: competition for paternal affection among the family's sons for the primary place in the family and the privileges this brings. In this case, both Jacob, ancestor of the entire people of Israel, and his son Joseph, ancestor of the northern tribes, incite the conflict. Jacob loves Joseph, ancestor of the northerners, more than his brothers, and he gives Joseph a long robe to express his affection (37:3). Joseph himself has dreams that give him authority over his brothers (37:5-10). Both experiences suggest to Joseph a privileged place in the family, even though the birthright was not his. His older brothers become understandably jealous and angry and plan to kill him (37:4, 8, 11, 18-20). A rift has opened in the people of Israel between the northerners, Joseph's descendants, who, in fact, hold Israel's best and richest land, and the rest of the tribes of Israel. And that rift almost becomes deadly.

This conflict among Israel's tribes is as complicated as the one between Isaac and Ishmael and the one between Jacob and Esau. The Storyteller, again, refuses to take sides. He does not present the conflict between the different parties as a simple matter of right and wrong, good and bad. Conflict across differences is never simple. We sympathize with Joseph's brothers who feel wronged by their father's favoritism and who feel insulted by their younger brother Joseph's brash pride. We would feel that way too. But we are horrified by the deadly revenge plotted by his brothers. We feel great relief when Joseph's life is spared, and we grieve for the young boy sold into slavery in a foreign land. We despair that such a shattered relationship can ever be repaired.

Both the Storyteller and the Northern Storyteller preserve traditions about the attempt to annihilate the hated brother, traditions that have been woven together almost seamlessly. In the Northern Storyteller's version, Reuben, Jacob's oldest son, averts catastrophe. In this version, Joseph's brothers plan to kill him and throw his body into a desert cistern. Reuben intercedes on Joseph's behalf, convincing his brothers not to kill him but to throw Joseph in the cistern alive. Reuben himself plans to return to rescue him. Before Reuben can return, Midianite traders find Joseph, rescue him, take him with them to Egypt, and sell him to the Egyptians. Reuben, finding the cistern empty, thinks Joseph is dead (37:19-22, 24, 28a, 29-30, 36). However, according to the Storyteller's version, it is Judah, Jacob's primary heir and David's ancestor, who averts catastrophe and saves Joseph. When Joseph's brothers plan to kill him, Judah intercedes on Joseph's behalf, convincing his brothers to sell Joseph to Ishmaelite traders passing by, who take Joseph with them to sell him to the Egyptians. When the brothers return to their father, they convince Jacob that Joseph has been killed by a wild animal (37:18, 23, 25-27, 28b, 31-35).

In the narrative that follows, two heroes emerge to create the future. They face the conflict over status and privilege, engage it directly, and forge paths forward that allow all their brothers to flourish. In the story's larger meaning, these heroes make space for all their descendants, the tribes of Israel, to live together with their differences. The first of these heroes is Judah, the ancestor of David's southern tribe. He has already acted to prevent the death of Joseph, ancestor of the two most powerful northern tribes. In the narratives that follow, Judah assumes leadership in the family. He takes charge of buying grain from Egypt to keep his brothers alive during the years of famine (43:1-5; 46:28). In Egypt, he negotiates with Joseph for his brothers' safety (44:16). He protects Benjamin, Joseph's full brother, for whom his father Jacob has special affection, even offering to enslave himself to free Benjamin (43:8-10; 44:18-34). Viewed from the larger level of tribal meaning, Judah, surrogate for his descendant the Judahite David, saves the northern tribes from demise, rescues the remaining tribes from famine, and negotiates the conflict between the northern tribes (Joseph) and the remaining tribes (his brothers) to forge a new understanding between them and a way forward without recrimination, even sacrificing himself to do so. Certainly, the Storyteller is describing here the way King David, from the tribe of Judah, was able to bring together a diverse group of tribes, among whom conflicts were inevitable, into a single kingdom, a strong people, a proud ethnic community, that lasted over four hundred years.

The other hero is Joseph, ancestor of the two most powerful northern tribes, Ephraim and Manasseh. Like Esau, his uncle,

Joseph loses the primary role in his family. Though he is not born into that role, as was Esau, his father's favoritism has led him to anticipate it. Like Esau, in spite of his losses, he flourishes, so that when he meets his brothers again, he has gained a position of power over them. Like Esau, he has both the motive and the resources to take revenge, to even the score, to right the wrongs, and to put himself back in the place he believed he deserved. But he doesn't. He places his past mistreatment behind him and reconciles with his brothers. He places the importance of the kinship relationships in which he belongs above past tensions, conflicts, and mistreatment.

It is very important to recognize that in both the Jacob and Esau story and the story of Joseph and his brothers, it is not the weaker and more vulnerable party, Jacob in one case and Joseph's brothers in the other, who is required to put the past aside and plead for reconciliation. The one who acts is the person with power, who can fan the flames of conflict, who can continue the cycle of wrong and revenge, and who has good reason actually to even the score. It is the more powerful person who stops the cycle of conflict and who builds a new relationship across difference by being committed to the fundamental connections between the parties and to their common desire to survive and flourish. Both stories describe the responsible use of power to cross bridges and rebuild relationships.

In both cases, the individual who represents this commitment to relationships over the conflict that differences can cause and who possesses the power to build bridges is *not* the ancestor of the Storyteller's own people. In the story of Jacob and Esau, this leader through conflict is Esau, the ancestor of the Edomites. In the story of Joseph and his brothers, it is Joseph, the ancestor of the northern tribes, not of the southern tribe of Judah, to which the Storyteller likely belongs. Both narratives reveal an imagination in which Israel's own pedigree and ethnicity are established and legitimated, but in which others are given places of power, respect, generosity, and humanity. These others participate in powerful ways to address the conflict across ethnic differences, to construct new relationships, and to provide ways forward to flourish with difference.

Before completing our examination of the negotiation of ethnic identity and difference among Israel's tribal groups themselves represented by Jacob's sons, we should be sure to recognize Israel's own complex ethnic identity, using these two heroes as illustrations. Both Judah and Joseph marry outside of their kinship networks and therefore create tribal identities for their descendants that are themselves "bi-cultural." Some texts in Genesis express a preference for endogamy, marriage between close blood relatives, as we've already seen in the Priest's concern that Jacob not marry Hittite or Canaanite women (27:46–28:9). Yet Judah, the ancestor of King David himself and of the Storyteller's own tribe, marries a Canaanite woman (38:2), and then impregnates his daughter-in-law, Tamar, likely also a Canaanite, whose son from this union, Perez, becomes David's direct ancestor (34:29; Ruth 4:18-22; Matt 1:1-6). Joseph, our story's other hero, marries Asenath, an Egyptian priest's daughter, who gives birth to Ephraim and Manasseh, ancestors of the primary northern tribes. These heirs of Joseph are thus half Egyptian.

The great heroes at the end of Genesis, Judah and Joseph, both establish what we today would call bi-cultural families, and thus tribal identities, one Israelite-Canaanite and the other Israelite-Egyptian. In fact, we might even consider Joseph himself to assume a hybrid or bi-cultural identity (Gen 50:1-5). Raised in Egypt's culture, he takes a position of power within it and follows Egyptian customs at his father's death. When he returns to Canaan to bury his father Jacob, the Canaanites see him as an Egyptian, not as an Israelite (50:11).[2] Thus, as the book of Genesis

---

2. Jennifer J. Ikoma-Motzko, "Walk Like an (Israelite) Egyptian: Genesis 50:1-26," in *The Beginning of Difference: How the Authors of Genesis Thought about Themselves and Others*, ed. Theodore Hiebert (Chicago: McCormick Theological Seminary, 2012), 254–82.

comes to a conclusion with its last generation, the generation that represents the internal groups that define Israel itself, Genesis's authors, in particular the Storyteller himself, recognize the complexity of Israel's own ethnic identity. They recognize in their own community a fundamental aspect of all ethnicities: they are not homogeneous, static, and unchangeable but flexible, changing, and complex. Israel's own identity at the end of Genesis incorporates individuals and cultural dimensions of other cultures. It draws into itself real elements of the difference within which it lives and evolves.

Canaan

The broad narrative cycles of Isaac and Ishmael, Jacob and Esau, and Joseph and his brothers dominate the book of Genesis, and they lay out Israel's core ideas about living with difference. They reveal how Israel constructed, through its ancestral stories, its own identity and its relationship to others. We have not been able to explore Israel's relations with all its neighbors, the Egyptians, the Moabites and Ammonites, the Philistines, the Arameans, and the Shechemites, to name the major examples. We can see that these narratives confirm in substantial ways the views of identity and difference we encountered in broader family stories. One episode, however, is unique and anomalous in Genesis, and this is the Storyteller's account of Noah's curse on Canaan in Genesis 9:18-27.

The story of Canaan's curse is unique in almost every way. Its conflict is not ignited over a competition for the primary role in the family, but by Ham's sin against his father. No threat of death follows, and no resolution and restoration of relationships occur. Ham's son, Canaan, rather than Ham himself, receives Noah's curse: "Cursed be Canaan: the lowest servant he will be for his brothers" (9:25). This curse is the single exception to the character of the new world introduced by Noah, which was a world of righteousness and blessing for all. Unlike others in non-Israelite lineages in the great family stories, Canaan is not portrayed with the status and respect people like Ishmael and Esau are accorded. Canaan is not annihilated like Abel in the pre-flood era. He is made subservient to his brothers. But his curse makes him the only cursed individual and his descendants the only cursed community. They are the exception to the nuanced view of others in all these post-flood stories. Why? What is the Storyteller saying about difference in this exceptional episode?

The only way to address these questions is to retrieve as best we can the historical circumstances behind Canaan's curse. According to biblical history, the great conflict through which Israel established itself as a distinct ethnic group in the Mediterranean highlands at the beginning of the first millennium BCE was its bitter conflict with the Canaanites. In the books of Joshua and Judges, the Canaanite wars are portrayed as the conflict between outsider Israelites and indigenous Canaanites. Archaeologists have shown, however, that the Israelites in their origins were actually indigenous Canaanites themselves. In the earliest settlements attributed to them, their material culture arises from Canaan itself, not from outside influences.[3] So, we must actually view the conflict between Israelites and Canaanites as a struggle between closely related peoples for distinct identities within the same land and out of the same cultural legacy.

However we look at the origin of this conflict, it was apparently so formative in Israel's struggle to establish its own identity that it was never forgotten. It assumed a kind of frozen moment and iconic place in Israel's social memory and in its genealogical history. The Storyteller does not abandon the claim that Israel and Canaan were related as part of Noah's global family tree. He still includes the Canaanites within this kinship structure of

---

3. Lawrence E. Stager, "The Archaeology of the Family in Ancient Israel," *Bulletin of the American Schools of Oriental Research* 260 (1985): 1–35.

relatedness. In fact, the Storyteller's central hero in Genesis, the figure of Judah from whom King David descends, marries a Canaanite. Nevertheless, this primal experience of conflict remains so strong that the Storyteller establishes an unusually strong boundary between the Israelites and Canaanites through an important genealogical move. Instead of recognizing the Canaanites as the close relatives they actually are by making them close relatives like the Ishmaelites and Edomites, the Storyteller places them as early as possible in his genealogy, as a grandson of Noah at the very beginning of his family tree. He makes them an excessively distant relative, and he considers them cursed with servitude under Israelite hegemony. This is the most negative image of others in Genesis, and it is important not as representative of the Storyteller's view of difference but as uniquely anomalous.

Because of Canaan's curse, he has been used in the United States to legitimate the most virulent oppression of others, in particular, the justification of slavery and segregation of African peoples.[4] This use of Canaan's story, even granting the story's problematic character, is entirely an act of misinterpretation of a biblical text. In the first place, this story is about the Canaanites in particular, not about any other peoples in the Storyteller's world. Only Canaan is cursed, not the rest of Ham's descendants, with whom later racist interpreters have connected the curse. The Storyteller connects none of Ham's other descendants with Canaan's curse. Even if we were to look dimly on Ham's descendants because of their father's act, which the Storyteller does not do, they cannot be narrowly equated with the people of North Africa but represent instead peoples from Canaan, Mesopotamia, Arabia, Egypt, and Libya. Finally, the racist use in the United States of Canaan's curse in Genesis violates the basic embrace of ethnic identity and ethnic differences as God's design for the world held by Genesis's authors. It violates the vision of difference based in

---

4. Stephen R. Haynes, *Noah's Curse: The Biblical Justification of American Slavery* (Oxford: Oxford University Press, 2002).

relatedness that Noah's family tree represents. And it violates the recognition and respect for others that the great family stories in Genesis affirm.

Living with Difference

In their great family narratives in the book of Genesis, the Storyteller, the Northern Storyteller, and the Priest display imaginations about living with difference that are realistic, generous, and optimistic. By beginning these stories with conflict, the authors of Genesis are, of course, great and skilled storytellers, capturing the attention of their listeners and creating the dramatic tension around which the stories rise to their crescendo and resolve themselves. By beginning with conflict, Genesis's authors, at the same time, express their realism about living with difference. They know by experience the tensions that can develop between parties who are different, whether they be brothers in a family, subgroups within a single ethnicity (as were the tribes of Israel), or peoples on an "international" stage (as were the Israelites and their neighbors the Ishmaelites and the Edomites). They know that violence and annihilation are constant threats to resolve difference. They consider erasure of others an ever-present danger. That is the lesson of the story of Cain and Abel. They understand the high stakes of difference.

In spite of their sober realism, and probably also because of it, they cultivate broad and generous imaginations about living with difference. The foundation of this generous imagination is the conception of kinship, which places all differences and distinctions within a framework of relatedness. Such an imagination does not begin with the idea of outsiders and insiders or of exclusion and inclusion. It begins with the idea of relationship and connection as the fundamental reality in which we all live. Genealogies and genealogical narratives are, as Eviatar Zerubavel reminds us, "visions of relatedness."[5] The biblical imagination provides a foundation for thinking of others as part of our family, as belonging to our network of relatives, as sharing our common humanity. It provides a powerful and positive place to begin thinking about difference.

By viewing others as members of their own family, Genesis's authors also recognize others as occupying an authentic and legitimate place in God's world and sharing the divine care that they themselves experience. They are all part of Noah's family tree, and they all share in the new age of righteousness and blessing that Noah inaugurated. Others are not outside of God's designs and God's protection. Even though sent away from Abraham's household, Hagar and Ishmael are the focus of God's care in the story about them, and they receive the very promises of blessing and success that Abraham and Isaac, Israel's own ancestors, receive. Ishmael and Esau (Edom) are portrayed as fully human, Esau even as Jacob's generous protector. Genesis's authors tell Israel's own story, of course, and give most time and space to Israel's relationship with God and the blessings that flow from this relationship. But they do not thereby exclude others from God's care, or delegitimize their place in God's diverse world, or dehumanize them. They possess an imagination in which difference is normal. And they invest great positive energy in creating narrative models for living in a world of difference where both they themselves and others will flourish.

Finally, Genesis's authors have cultivated imaginations of optimism. Though they understand deeply the high stakes of difference and the threat of conflict, they are not pessimists. Their stories imagine a world in which conflict is negotiated successfully, in which the demeaning, exclusion, and erasure of others is averted, and in which differences flourish. They tell stories in which they legitimate, celebrate, and take pride in their own genealogical history and identity. And in these same stories, they legitimate,

5. Eviatar Zerubavel, *Ancestors and Relatives*, xi.

respect, and honor the genealogical history and identity of others in their diverse world. They reveal broad and constructive imaginations for living with difference. After generations and generations of history, they remain important conversation partners for us today, we who are still finding ways to forge positive futures in God's diverse world.

Pentecost: The First Christians Embrace Difference

The author of Luke-Acts turns to ethnic discourse, to the consideration of human differences not as obstacles to unity to be transcended but theologically vibrant sites for God's action in the world.

—Eric Barreto, "Negotiating Difference: Theology and Ethnicity in the Acts of the Apostles"[1]

In chapters 1–3 of this book, we looked in a fresh way at the attitudes concerning identity and difference, which were held by the authors who wrote Israel's earliest history. In these Genesis narratives about the beginning of difference, we discovered a deep appreciation for ethnic particularity and social solidarity. These texts exhibit a true acceptance of difference and offer creative ways to embrace it and negotiate it. This acceptance of difference included the recognition of difference as the norm for life in this world (chapter 1), a deep interest in understanding Israel's relationship with those who were different from them as part of a common family (chapter 2), and a respect for those who are different, which does not stereotype them, erase them, or make them inferior (chapter 3). These biblical narratives affirm

---

1. Eric D. Barreto, "Negotiating Difference," 131.

difference as God's intention for the world in which Israel shaped its own identity.

In this chapter, we move forward from the world of the ancient Israelite community to the first-century world of the early Christian community, for which these narratives were scripture. The first century actually witnessed the birth of two great religions descended from ancient Israel—rabbinic Judaism and Christianity.[2] Both religions shared the common scripture that contained these stories of identity and difference in Genesis. And in each of these religions, these scriptural stories about identity and difference reverberate in both common and distinctive ways among Jewish and Christian Bible interpreters. The entire legacy of how Jews and Christians shared interpretations or marked out their distinctive paths is a story too long to tell here.

In this chapter, we focus on one important way in which these narratives from Genesis influenced the theology of early Christianity and its view of the church. We discover how an ancient scriptural narrative about difference influenced the nature of the church at its very origins. Ancient interpreters noticed almost immediately a connection between the story of Pentecost in Acts 2 and the story of Babel in Genesis 11. If there is a real connection, the relationship between these stories should tell us a lot about the way in which the early church defined itself at Pentecost and how it thought about identity and difference within early Christianity.

Pentecost: The Church's Charter

The events of Pentecost in Acts 2:1-13 describe the birth of the church.[3] Any story of origins aims to explain the reality in which its writer lives. As such, the Pentecost story of the church's beginning provides a kind of charter, a definition of what the

2. Alan F. Segal, *Rebecca's Children: Judaism and Christianity in the Roman World* (Cambridge, MA: Harvard University Press, 1986), 1.

3. Richard I. Pervo, *Acts*, Hermeneia (Minneapolis: Fortress, 2009), 70.

church is, and a preview of what the church is to become. It is a defining moment. It sets into place the identity of the church and its role in the world. What we find in this story about identity and difference will tell us a lot about the perspectives in the earliest Christian movement about ethnic identity and cultural difference and about how these perspectives determined the nature of the church in future centuries.

How the Pentecost story plays this role as the church's charter can be seen best by locating this story within its context in the Christian scriptures. The story itself is a key episode in the larger narrative made up of the two-volume work containing the Gospel of Luke and the book of Acts. From earliest times, interpreters regarded these two books as part of a single narrative describing the origins of Christianity, partly because they are addressed to the same person, the most honorable Theophilus (Luke 1:3; Acts 1:1) and also because they reflect a unity of structure, style, and thought. Within Luke-Acts, the author divides early Christianity into two periods, marked by appearances of the Holy Spirit. The first era is the period of Jesus's ministry, inaugurated by the descent of the Holy Spirit at Jesus's baptism (Luke 3:21-22). The second era is the period of the church and its ministry, inaugurated by the descent of the Holy Spirit a second time at Pentecost (Acts 2:1-13).[4] Thus, the Pentecost story creates the new Christian movement in much the same way that the Babel story created the new world after the flood.

The author of this comprehensive account of early Christianity, including its Pentecost narrative, is anonymous, though many scholars refer to him as Luke, as I will do here, out of deference to early interpreters who connected this two-volume work with Luke, the companion of Paul (Phil 24; Col 4:14). Luke appears to be a well-educated Gentile-Greek author who lived outside of Palestine in one of the areas of the Roman world to which the

---

4. Dennis C. Duling, *The New Testament: History, Literature, and Social Context,* 4th ed. (Belmont, CA: Thomson Wadsworth, 2003), 379.

church spread from its origin in Jerusalem at Pentecost. He wrote his account of Christian origins in the Greek language to other Gentile Greek-speaking Christians like himself throughout the Roman world, in order to legitimate their place in the Christian movement and also to legitimate the place of the Christian movement itself within the Roman Empire.

Luke's extensive knowledge of the Hebrew scriptures through their Greek translation in the Septuagint tells us that he may well have been a convert to Judaism, just like the converts at Pentecost (Acts 2:10), before he joined the Christian movement. He makes it clear—and this is one of the main themes of the Pentecost story itself—that Christianity originated in Judaism and that its Jewish roots formed a core part of its identity as it spread into the Gentile world. In fact, we might summarize Luke's aim in writing Luke-Acts as demonstrating how Christianity spread from its Jewish origins in Jerusalem at Pentecost to all corners of the Gentile Roman Empire and even to Rome itself. Jesus's final words as Luke records them are: "You will receive power when the Holy Spirit has come upon you, and you will be my witnesses in Jerusalem, in all Judea and Samaria, and to the end of the earth" (Acts 1:8).

Pentecost Reverses Babel

We are most interested in how Luke thought about identity and difference while he describes the movement of Christianity from a single culture and language and place into multiple cultures and languages and places throughout the world. And we are especially interested in how he thought about identity and difference in his account of the church's charter at its birth in Jerusalem at Pentecost. Even more particularly, we want to know how Luke may have used the story of Babel to shape his story of Pentecost. But before we engage Luke's Pentecost story in detail and his use of the story of Babel as a source for his story, we must acknowledge the way in which Christian interpreters through time have read Luke's account of Pentecost in relation to Babel. Just as I've challenged the traditional reading of the Babel story and its views of identity and difference in chapter 1, I challenge here the usual way Christians read the Pentecost story and understand its views of identity and difference.

From the beginning of early Christian thought, interpreters and theologians recognized a connection between Luke's account of Pentecost and the story of Babel in Genesis. St. Augustine, for example, writing in the fourth century, describes the Babel-Pentecost relationship as it has been viewed throughout Christian history. In his commentary on Psalm 55, he writes, "Through proud men, divided were the tongues; through humble Apostles, united were the tongues. Spirit of pride dispersed tongues; Holy Spirit united tongues."[5] And in a sermon on the Gospel of John, he says, "If pride caused diversities of tongues, Christ's humility has united these diversities in one. The Church is now bringing together what the tower had sundered. Of one tongue there were made many... of many tongues there is made one."[6]

Augustine's interpretation makes two important moves that reflect the traditional understanding of Pentecost throughout the church's history. First, he understands the diversity of languages at Babel not as God's intention for the world (as proposed in chapter 1) but as God's punishment for pride (as most interpreters of Genesis have assumed). He therefore views the different languages that Babel introduced as a problem that needs to be solved. Second, he believes the solution to the problem of difference is unity, and unity is reintroduced at Pentecost. Many languages become one again. What the tower tore apart, the church brings together. What Babel broke, Pentecost fixes. The difference that Babel

---

5.   St. Augustine, "Psalm LV," in *A Select Library on the Nicene and Post-Nicene Fathers of the Christian Church*, vol. VIII, *St. Augustine: Exposition of the Book of Psalms*, ed. P. Schaff (Grand Rapids, MI: Eerdmans, 1996), 213.

6.   St. Augustine, "Tractate VI," in *A Select Library on the Nicene and Post-Nicene Fathers of the Christian Church*, vol. VII, *St. Augustine: Homilies on the Gospel of John; Soliloquies*, ed. P. Schaff (Grand Rapids, MI: Eerdmans, 1991), 42.

inflicted on the world is overcome by unity at Pentecost. The unity Augustine sees in Pentecost is clearly the single gospel that is preached, and to emphasize this Augustine effectively focuses our reading of Pentecost not on difference but on uniformity, not on diversity but on unity. Pentecost's charter for the church is unity.

Augustine's view that Pentecost reversed Babel by overcoming difference through unity is the way he himself had learned to read the story, and it is still the way we learn to read Pentecost today. One contemporary commentator refers to Luke's Pentecost story as "A Reversal of Babel."[7] Another writes that "by reversing linguistic diversity, the experience [of Pentecost] is revealed as . . . a utopian restoration of the unity of the human race."[8] The view that Pentecost preaches unity is perpetuated not just in the best and most exhaustive commentaries on Acts but in the church's communication to the world. The Second Vatican Council in its document on missions, for example, describes Pentecost this way: "The union (of all peoples) was to be achieved by the Church of the New Covenant, a church which speaks all tongues, and thus overcomes the divisiveness of Babel (at Pentecost)."[9] Oneness, not difference, has become the key theme of Pentecost. Transcending difference, not engaging and affirming difference, has become Pentecost's definition of the church.

Pentecost Builds on Babel

This chapter challenges our traditional way of reading the story of Pentecost by making four proposals. The first is that Luke knew the story of Babel in Genesis 11 well. This is not hard to establish because we can see how well Luke knew the Hebrew scriptures by the way he referred to them extensively throughout

---

7. Craig S. Keener, *Acts: An Exegetical Commentary*, vol. 1 (Grand Rapids, MI: Baker Academic, 2012), 842.

8. Pervo, *Acts*, 61–62.

9. W. M. Abbott, SJ, ed., *The Documents of Vatican II* (London: Geoffrey Chapman, 1966), 588.

Luke-Acts. The second proposal is that Luke used the story of Babel in Genesis 11 as a source for his composition of the Pentecost story in Acts 2. This too is not hard to establish, since, as we have already noted, ancient and modern commentators alike see a connection between these two narratives. Contemporary scholars suggest other sources for Luke as well, such as the Sinai episode in Exodus with its visitation of God in fire. And they have debated how much Luke actually relied on Babel for his Pentecost narrative. In this chapter, I will propose that Luke knew Babel well and relied on it extensively for his story of Pentecost. The story of Babel and the story of Pentecost are, after all, the only two stories of the diversification of language in the Bible, and language is the major theme in both.

The third proposal I wish to make is that Luke interpreted the story of Babel positively, in much the same way the authors of Genesis interpreted the story of Babel in chapter 1. Accordingly, Luke read Babel as a positive story about the reconstruction of cultural identity after the flood, and he viewed God's diversification of languages and dispersal of peoples around the world as God's intention for the world in the new post-flood era. This point is much more challenging to establish, given our traditional way of reading Pentecost. By Luke's time, understanding Babel as a story of pride and punishment had already become known among both Jewish and Christian interpreters. I aim to show that Luke read Babel differently from this more popular way of reading the story. Luke was an independent thinker who read Babel closely and distinctively as a positive narrative of difference.

The fourth proposal is that Luke modeled Pentecost on Babel. As a member of the diverse and cosmopolitan Mediterranean world, he understood the diverse cultures God created at Babel, which he experienced in the world around him, not as a punishment or a tragedy but as God's intention for the world, just as the author of the story of Babel understood. As a member of the Christian movement, which itself was becoming increasingly diverse, he composed the story of the church's birth at Pentecost to show how the church embraced from the beginning the diversity God creates in the world. Thus, unlike many of his peers, Luke saw Pentecost not in contrast with Babel but in continuity with it. And he wrote a charter for the church in which the world's difference would be the norm and in which the identities of its different cultures would be respected and affirmed in the church.

To show how Luke did this, we will take a fresh look at the details of the story of Pentecost, and we will focus on the way in which the details build positively on the story of Babel. The Pentecost story has two parts, as does the story of Babel. The first part of the Pentecost story, Acts 2:1-4, focuses on the followers of Jesus who, after his death, had gathered together in Jerusalem. It describes the Holy Spirit's descent to teach them other languages. The second part of the story of Pentecost, Acts 2:5-13, focuses on the crowd of people in Jerusalem from every nation under heaven. It describes them hearing Jesus's followers speaking to them in the different languages taught by the Holy Spirit. We begin by a close examination of the first part of the Pentecost story.

The Church Begins in Jerusalem: Acts 2:1-4

¹When Pentecost Day arrived, they were all together in one place. ²Suddenly a sound from heaven like the howling of a fierce wind filled the entire house where they were sitting. ³They saw what seemed to be individual flames of fire alighting on each one of them. ⁴They were all filled with the Holy Spirit and began to speak in other languages as the Spirit enabled them to speak.

Luke opens his account of the church's birth at Pentecost by introducing the three themes that will shape his entire story and his charter for the church: place, language, and identity. Luke begins his story by telling us that the first Christians "were all together in one place" (2:1). He goes on to describe the way these first Christians, who all spoke one language, were able to speak in many languages (2:2-4). And Luke focuses on the first Christians' common identity: gathered in one place, speaking a common language, Jesus's followers were devout Galilean Jews who prepared to celebrate the Jewish festival of Pentecost. Luke thus presents the earliest Christians as a single cultural community: a people with a common identity, speaking a common language, gathered in one place. Just how Luke builds this Pentecost narrative of the church's birth on his knowledge and understanding of the Babel story in Genesis 11 can be seen best if we provide here the first part of the story of Babel for comparison.

> [1]All people* on earth had one language and the same words. [2]When they traveled east, they found a valley in the land of Shinar and settled there. [3]They said to each other, "Come, let's make bricks and bake them hard." They used bricks for stones and asphalt for mortar. [4]They said, "Come, let's build for ourselves a city and a tower with its top in the sky, and let's make a name for ourselves so that we won't be dispersed over all the earth." [5]Then the LORD came down to see the city and the tower that the humans built. [6]And the LORD said, "There is now one people and they all have one language."
> *Hebrew lacks *people*

Let's review briefly the aim of the first half of the Babel story that Luke had in front of him. The Storyteller opened his story of Babel in Genesis not to describe an act of pride, as commonly thought, but to describe the first effort to reconstitute human community after the flood. In this effort, the world's first people, speaking one language, set about establishing their own cultural identity (making a name for themselves) by building a city and putting down roots in one place. When God descends, just as the Holy Spirit will do in the Pentecost story, God encounters a single cultural community: "one people" (a common descent group with a single identity), speaking "one language," gathered in one place.

The Storyteller thus recognizes the core human need for identity as a member of a distinctive ethnic community, and he describes the first human efforts to establish one. His key markers for such a community are language, place, and identity.

One Place: Jerusalem

To illustrate how Luke built his understanding of the church as a community on the Storyteller's account of the world's first community, let's examine each of these three cultural markers—language, place, and identity—one by one. And let's begin with place, since Luke begins his story by saying that at the church's birth the first Christians "were all together in one place." And let's lay the foundation for Luke's account by reviewing the role of place in the Babel story. There, place takes up most of the story's first part. The world's first people, speaking a common language, find a site to settle down (Gen 11:2) and construct an impressive city with a tower (11:3-4) to establish their residency and their identity in that one place (11:4). In the second half of the story, we find out that this is the city of Babel and that Babel is the one place from which all the peoples of the world spread out (11:8-9).

Luke begins his story with all Jesus's followers, just like the world's first people, gathered in one place. And for Luke too that place is a city, Jerusalem (Acts 2:5). Jerusalem is the site of the climactic events in Jesus's ministry: his Last Supper, his trial, his execution and burial, his resurrection and postresurrection appearances (Luke 22–24), and his ascent into heaven (Acts 1:9). Jerusalem is the place Jesus tells his followers to wait for the descent of the Holy Spirit (Acts 1:4, 12). Jerusalem is the place where Jesus tells his followers they would first preach his message (Luke 24:47; Acts 1:8). And Jerusalem is the one place from which the entire church will spread out: "You will be my witnesses in Jerusalem," Jesus tells his followers, "in all Judea and Samaria, and to the end of the earth" (Acts 1:8). Just as the world's first people begin their history in one city, so the church's first members begin their history in one city.

One Language: Aramaic

Luke introduces a second theme at the beginning of the Pentecost story: the theme of language, the other important defining marker of cultural identity in the Babel story. In fact, the theme of language dominates the first part of Luke's story. Again, let's lay the foundation for Luke's use of this theme by reviewing the role of language in the Babel story that Luke had in front of him. There, language has a preeminent role. The Storyteller begins his story of the world's first people forming their first community by describing their language: "All people on the earth had one language and the same words" (Gen 11:1). When God descends to engage the world's first community, the first thing God notices is their common language: "There is now one people and they all have one language" (11:6). And in the second half of the story, we find out that language is the first thing God diversifies to create the world's different cultures (11:7-9).

Just as in the story of Babel, language plays a leading role in the Pentecost narrative. It fills the first part of Luke's story like the sound that filled the house where Jesus's followers sat waiting (Acts 2:2). Luke begins his story with the world's first Christians, just like the world's first people, speaking a common language. In Luke's story, that common language was Aramaic. By the first century BCE, Aramaic had replaced Hebrew as the vernacular language in Palestine. It was the language that Jesus and his first followers spoke. It was, therefore, the common language of the earliest Christians gathered together in Jerusalem. It was the single language with which the early church began.

While Luke's earliest Christian community speaks a common language just as the world's first people do, Luke uses his Babel source creatively at this point. Luke introduces God's multiplication of languages in the first part of his narrative rather than waiting till the second part as the Storyteller does in Genesis 11. Even in his creative adaptation, however, Luke follows the Babel story closely. Just as God descends from heaven at Babel to diversify the world's languages (Gen 11:7), so the Holy Spirit descends at Pentecost to diversify the Christian community's languages (Acts 2:2, 4). Luke symbolizes and prefigures the Holy Spirit's descent already in verse 2 with the rushing wind that fills the house where Jesus's followers are gathered. The Greek terms *pnoēs*, "wind," in 2:2 and *pneumatos*, "Spirit," in 2:4 are related and can both mean wind, thus connecting the rushing wind with the Holy Spirit. In both stories, linguistic diversity begins with God. Difference is God's work and God's intention.

Luke describes the multiplication of languages in the earliest Christian community gathered in Jerusalem in 2:3 as "individual flames of fire alighting on each one of them." While fire is a common sign of divine appearances, as it was at Mount Sinai when the Instruction (*torah*) was given (Exod 19:16-18), Luke's attention here is on the flames resting on each person gathered together. "Flames" translates the Greek word *glōssa*, literally "tongue." When Luke uses the same Greek term *glōssa* for the other "languages" ("tongues") the Holy Spirit teaches each person in 2:4, he connects these languages with the flames of the Spirit. Thus, the first thing Luke tells us about the birth of the church is that the Holy Spirit diversified the single language of its first members into the languages of all the nations under heaven (Acts 2:4, 5, 7). Just as God introduced all the world's languages at Babel, so the Holy Spirit prompted the first Christians to speak them at Pentecost.

One Culture: Judaism

The third major theme Luke introduces at the beginning of the Pentecost story is the theme of cultural identity, another key defining mark of the world's first people in the Babel story. Once again, let's lay the foundation for Luke's treatment of this theme by reviewing the role identity plays in the Babel story that Luke had before him. There, the world's first people's efforts to build a distinctive cultural community with its own ethnic identity are captured in their words "let's make a name for ourselves" (Gen 11:4), since "name" in the ancient biblical world signified one's identity, particularity, and reputation. Among the people at Babel, sharing a common language and a common place were the key markers of their common identity, as they were, in fact, throughout the ancient world.

For Luke too the first Christians' language and their place—their Aramaic language and their residency in Jerusalem—were key markers of their common culture and distinctive ethnic identity. Luke, though, tells us even more about their identity. They were devout Jews who were in Jerusalem to celebrate Pentecost (2:1). Pentecost means "fiftieth," the name Greek-speaking Jews gave to the Festival of Weeks, held a week of weeks or fifty days after Passover. Originally an agricultural festival celebrating the late grain harvest, Pentecost became associated with Moses's reception of the Torah on Mount Sinai. The most devout Jews, when they could, celebrated the primary Jewish religious festivals in Jerusalem itself (2:5). When he located the birth of the church among devout Jews celebrating one of their great religious festivals, Luke highlights the Jewish identity of the first Christians and the Jewish roots of the new Christian movement.

Luke is even more specific about the distinctive identity of these first Jewish Christians. They represent not all Jews but those particular Jews who were followers of Jesus. They saw in Jesus the fulfillment of their prophets' hopes (Acts 2:16; 7:42; 8:28), and they believed Jesus to be the embodiment of their future. As such, they were a tiny group within the larger Jewish community. When Luke calls them Galileans, he identifies their common geographical origins: they are Jews from the Galilee, the northern part of Palestine where much of Jesus's ministry took place and from which his first followers came (Acts 2:7; compare 1:11, 12 and Luke 22:59 and Luke 23:5, 49, 55). Luke counts among them the eleven disciples (Acts 1:13-14), in addition to Mattathias elected in Judas's place (1:26), some women and Jesus's mother and brothers (1:13-14), and 120 believers (1:15).

Luke, therefore, begins the history of the church like the history of the world: with a single culture. The world begins with a small community that speaks a common language, moves to one place to build a city, and sets about creating the world's first distinctive culture. Likewise, the church begins with a small community that shares a common language, Aramaic. With roots in the Galilee, they all gather in their central religious city of Jerusalem to celebrate Pentecost. They are devout Jews who are Jesus followers. Luke emphasizes these first Christians' cultural solidarity by beginning and ending the first part of his story with the word *all*: "they were *all* together in one place...they were *all* filled with the Holy Spirit" (Acts 2:1, 4). Earlier in his narrative, he had already spoken of this little community's solidarity: "a family of believers...united in their devotion to prayer" (1:14-15).

For Luke, the distinctive, singular, and deeply Jewish roots of the church are extremely important. Luke's overarching aim in Luke-Acts is to show how the church moved from its single culture of origin in Jerusalem out to the multiple cultures of the world. In Jesus's last instructions to his followers before his ascension, Jesus tells them, "you will receive power when the Holy Spirit has come upon you, and you will be my witnesses in Jerusalem, in all Judea and Samaria, and to the end of the earth" (Acts 1:8). When Luke documents the church's growing diversity and legitimates its Gentile mission, he never rejects or criticizes the distinctive Jewish culture in which it is born. Luke honors the church's Jewish origins and ongoing Jewish character. Just as the Storyteller in Genesis respects the distinctive culture the first humans built after the flood as well as God's descent to diversify it, so Luke respects the distinctive culture of the first Christians and the Holy Spirit's descent to diversify it.

It seems probable that, like the world's citizens after the flood, this small Jewish community assembled in Jerusalem intends and expects their single cultural identity to endure and remain intact much as they knew it to be. When Jesus instructs his followers during his resurrection appearances to wait in Jerusalem for the arrival of the Holy Spirit and the church's beginning, they ask him, "Lord, are you going to restore the kingdom to Israel now?" (Acts 1:6). They are thinking of their future in terms of their past heritage as members of a Davidic dynasty located within the boundaries of ancient Israel and reassuming its role as a small self-standing kingdom in ancient West Asia. Like the people of Babel, the first Christians are comfortable and secure in their common life as they knew it to be. They don't see difference coming.

The Church Moves into the World: Acts 2:5-13

[5]There were pious Jews from every nation under heaven living in Jerusalem. [6]When they heard this sound, a crowd gathered. They were mystified because everyone heard them speaking in their native languages. [7]They were surprised and amazed, saying, "Look, aren't all the people who are speaking Galileans, every one of them? [8]How then can each of us hear them speaking in our native language? [9]Parthians, Medes, and Elamites; as well as residents of Mesopotamia, Judea, and Cappadocia, Pontus and Asia, [10]Phrygia and Pamphylia, Egypt and the regions of Libya bordering Cyrene; and visitors from Rome (both Jews and converts to Judaism), [11]Cretans and Arabs—we hear them declaring the mighty works of God in their own

languages!" ¹²They were all surprised and bewildered. Some asked each other, "What does this mean?" ¹³Others jeered at them, saying, "They're full of new wine!"

Luke continues his account of the church's birth at Pentecost by developing the three themes that shaped the church's charter in the first part of his story: place, language, and identity. While the church begins as a small, single cultural community gathered in one place and speaking one language, it explodes in the Pentecost story's second part into multiple cultural communities living in many places, speaking many languages. Luke builds the second part of his Pentecost narrative of the church's birth on the Babel story in Genesis 11, just as he built the first part of his Pentecost narrative on it. We can see this best if we review the second part of the story of Babel in Genesis 11 for comparison.

> ⁵Then the LORD came down to see the city and the tower that the humans built. ⁶And the LORD said, "There is now one people and they all have one language. This is what they have begun to do and now all that they plan to do will be possible for them. ⁷Come, let's go down and mix up [prepare a mixture of] their language there so they won't understand each other's language." ⁸Then the LORD dispersed them from there over all the earth, and they stopped building the city. ⁹Therefore, it is named Babel because there the LORD mixed up [prepared a mixture of] the language of all the earth; and from there the LORD dispersed them over all the earth.

Let's review briefly the aim of this second half of the Babel story that Luke had in front of him. Seeing that the world's first people after the flood had set about building their own single culture with one language in one place, God determines that the post-flood world will be multicultural. God, therefore, steps in to diversify the world's cultures by two actions: multiplying the languages people speak and dispersing them to different places across the world. God responds, as we've seen in chapter 1, not to punish the people for anything they've done or to introduce confusion into the world. Nor does God disapprove of the human desire for cultural identity as such. God simply determines that the world in which the Storyteller lives will be full of many cultural identities. In this way, the story of Babel explains for Luke the world around him, the world he describes in the second half of his Pentecost story. The world of difference Luke sees is the world he believes God intended and the world God created at Babel.

Many Places

It is just this diverse world Luke describes when he identifies those at Pentecost as people "from every nation under heaven" (Acts 2:5). Just as place and language are key markers of cultural identity in the first half of the Babel story and of cultural difference in the second half of the Babel story, so place and language are the key markers of cultural identity in the first half of Luke's Pentecost story and of cultural difference in the second half of the Pentecost story. Let's begin with place, because that is where Luke begins the second part of his story, just as he did its first part. And let's recall the role of place in the second part of the Babel story. There, the Storyteller tells us that to diversify the world's cultures, God disperses the world's first people to spread out and inhabit the entire earth. From the single city of Babel, God sends them out to settle all the world's lands: "From there the LORD dispersed them over all the earth" (Gen 11:7, 9).

This is exactly the "dispersed" world Luke describes in the beginning of the second half of his Pentecost story. He identifies those who experienced the Pentecost event as devout Jews "from every nation under heaven" (2:5). In fact, the long list of the world's nations from which these people come takes up major space in the second half of Luke's story (2:9-11). It is this list that lectionary readers still stumble over today when they read Luke's story of Pentecost. And that challenge is the point! The people who heard the message at Pentecost and who would receive the Christian message far and wide in Luke's day were citizens of a bewildering array of countries with names still difficult to pronounce. They were "from every nation under heaven." Luke wants to make it clear that the church born at Pentecost will mirror the diverse cultural world God created at Babel. While the Storyteller in Genesis doesn't name the diverse places to which God dispersed the people from Babel, Luke does so by naming fifteen concrete nations that map his world from one end to the other.

We can see how intent Luke was to model the church's diversity on the world's diversity by looking at the names of the peoples and places Luke uses to represent the people present at Pentecost. They prefigure the church's movement out from Jerusalem to the ends of the earth. Luke begins his survey of nations out on the far eastern frontier of the Roman Empire with the Parthian Empire, in the area of modern Iran, and with two of the peoples, the Medes and Elamites, who had historically inhabited these lands. He pulls back west to mention Mesopotamia, in the area of modern Iraq, and then Judea itself, in which Jerusalem was located. Then Luke turns north of Jerusalem to name key Roman provinces in ancient Anatolia, the area of modern Turkey. He names Cappadocia in the northeast, Pontus in the north on the Black Sea, Asia in the west on the Aegean Sea, Phrygia in the northwest, and Pamphylia in the southwest. Paul concentrated much of his missionary work in these places (Acts 13–14, 18–20). Then Luke turns south to northern Africa. He names Egypt, with a large Jewish community in Alexandria where the church would take root, and Cyrene, in the area of modern Libya, from which Simon, Jesus's cross bearer, came (Luke 23:26).

Finally, Luke looks west all the way to Rome itself, which holds the climactic geographical position in Luke's list of the world's people and places. Rome had organized the diverse cultures of Luke's day into a sprawling worldwide empire. But even more important for Luke, Rome was the final outpost, the ultimate destination in the movement of the church from Jerusalem, to Judea and Samaria, and to the end of the earth. It is the place to which the entire narrative of the church in Luke-Acts moves, the final location of Paul's missionary enterprise (Acts 28:11-31). Having named the westernmost reach of Christianity in Luke's day, he pulls back east toward Jerusalem to mention the Mediterranean island of Crete, just south of Greece, and the land of the Arabs, the ancient Nabatean Kingdom just east of Jerusalem, in the area of modern Jordan. As far as his own horizons would allow, Luke maps out the dispersed world of Babel that would become the habitation of the church born in Jerusalem at Pentecost.

Many Languages

Worldwide geographical diversity is just one of the key characteristics of Luke's church. The other is the diversity of its languages. In fact, Luke makes the multiplication of languages the most prominent feature of the Pentecost story, just as it is the most prominent feature of the Babel story that Luke adapts. To fully understand how Luke centers his attention on language, let's review briefly the crucial role language plays in the Babel story. The Storyteller's overall aim in Genesis 11 is to explain the profusion of the world's cultures around him, and to do so he focuses on language as culture's primary marker. The first thing he mentions about the world's first people's distinctive single culture is their one language (Gen 11:1). The first thing God notices about their building a common cultural identity is their one language (11:6). And the first thing God does to diversify human cultures is to diversify their one language (11:7, 9).

We've already seen how Luke makes God's introduction of different languages the central theme of the first part of his story of Pentecost (Acts 2:1-4). Just as God descends from heaven at Babel to enable the world's people to speak its different languages

(Gen 11:7), so the Holy Spirit descends at Pentecost to empower the first Christians to speak those languages (Acts 2:2, 4). The "individual flames of fire alighting on each one of them" symbolize these languages (2:3). Luke uses the same Greek term *glōssa* for the "flames" resting on each person in 2:3 and the "languages" the Holy Spirit taught each person in 2:4. Thus, the first thing Luke tells us about the new church is that the Holy Spirit enabled its first members to speak all the languages of all the nations under heaven (Acts 2:4, 5, 7). Just as God introduced all the world's languages at Babel, so the Holy Spirit taught the first Christians to speak all them at Pentecost. In both stories, linguistic diversity begins with God. Difference is God's work and God's intention.

Worldwide linguistic diversity is the other key characteristic of Luke's charter for the church. Just as it dominates the first part of the story of Pentecost, so the speaking of many languages dominates the second part of the story. When Luke's narrative shifts scenes from the small homogenous gathering in part one (2:1-4) to the large diverse crowd gathered outside in part two (2:5-13), the one single event—the only event!—Luke describes is what the crowd hears. And what each person in the crowd hears is Jesus's followers speaking to them in their own native language. Luke repeats this three times. First, he tells us that this happened: "each one heard them speaking in the native language of each" (2:6 NRSV). Then he quotes the crowd saying this. Twice. "Are not all these who are speaking Galileans? And how is it that we hear, each of us, in our own native language?" (2:7-8 NRSV). "In our own languages we hear them speaking about God's deeds of power" (2:11 NRSV). This is the one big thing that happened at Pentecost. It's really the *only thing* that happened at Pentecost. Each person present heard about God's powerful deeds, *in their own native language.* The church born at Pentecost is a multilingual church.

The people in the crowd, who come from all parts of Luke's world, respond with sheer wonderment at all this multilingualism.

Luke outdoes himself to emphasize the people's surprise. Luke tells us that the members of the crowd are "mystified" (2:6), "surprised and amazed" (2:7), and "surprised and bewildered" (2:12). They can't believe it. All their mystification, their bewilderment, their surprise, and their amazement reveal just how unexpected this outburst of different languages was to them. At one level, they don't expect Galilean Jews to know these different languages. But at another deeper level, they don't expect difference to be the hallmark of the future church. As we've already seen, Jesus's followers expected Jesus to renew the single distinctive culture in which they were members when they gathered in Jerusalem (1:6). They don't see difference coming. Now Luke makes it clear that people from around the world react in the same way. They don't expect the message of Jesus to be translatable into the indigenous languages and cultures of their world. That's why some just think Jesus's followers were drunk (2:13). It's why others ask, "What does this mean?" (2:12). It meant, of course, that the church would embrace difference!

Luke doesn't name the various native languages the crowd gathered at Pentecost heard Jesus's followers speak to them. He just names their countries (2:9-11). But we know from historical records that many regional languages in these areas remained important throughout the Roman Empire, even though Latin and Greek, the language of Luke-Acts itself, were its official languages. Parthian, an ancient northwestern Iranian language, was spoken by the Parthians, Medes, and Elamites. Aramaic and Syriac were important languages in Mesopotamia. Aramaic, the language of Jesus's followers themselves, was the regional language of Judea. Cappadocian and Phrygian were regional languages in ancient Anatolia, modern Turkey, as well as Galatian, Psidian, Mysian, and Isaurian, in the areas of Pontus, Asia, and Pamphylia. Coptic was the regional indigenous language of Egypt. Ancient Afroasiatic languages such as Numidian and Berber were spoken in the parts of Libya belonging to Cyrene. Latin was the primary language in

Rome. While he is writing his story of Pentecost in Greek, one of the Roman Empire's official languages, it's the regional languages such as these that Luke has in mind when he says that the crowd heard Jesus's followers speaking in their own native languages.

As we've already seen in our analysis of the stories of Babel and Pentecost, language is one of the most foundational aspects of culture. In most cultures, "language is the intimate, articulate expression of culture," writes Lamin Sanneh, professor of Missions and World Christianity, "and so close are the two that language can be said to be commensurate with culture, which it suffuses and embodies."[10] By making language their main theme, both stories thus declare their central interest in cultural identity and difference. And both stories aim to understand and interpret the importance of cultural identity within the radical pluralism of the world's cultures.

In their quest to engage difference through the theme of language, the stories of Babel and Pentecost both validate the distinctive ethnic identity of individual cultures, on the one hand, and the radical diversity of these individual cultures in the world, on the other. And both do so by attributing to God the distinctive ethnic identities that make up the world's different cultures. At Babel, God acts to diversify the languages of the world's original inhabitants after the flood in order to create the cultural diversity in which the Storyteller of Babel himself lived. At Pentecost, the Holy Spirit acts to diversify the languages of Jesus's followers to create the multicultural church in which Luke himself is a member. "The author of Luke-Acts," says Eric Barreto, "turns to ethnic discourse, to the consideration of human differences not as obstacles to unity to be transcended but theologically vibrant sites for God's action in the world."[11]

---

10. Lamin Sanneh, *Translating the Message: The Missionary Impact on Culture*, rev. ed. (Maryknoll, NY: Orbis Books, 2009), 3.

11. Barreto, *"Negotiating Difference,"* 131.

In the Pentecost narrative, the act of translation itself, by which Jesus's followers translated their message from Aramaic into the various indigenous languages of the Roman Empire, carries with it a deep respect for difference and its indigenous cultures. Sanneh forcefully argues that the very process of language translation acknowledges the inherent value of the indigenous culture, affirms its identity, and recognizes it as the agent of religious interpretation and practice. Translation assumes "the recipient culture as a valid and necessary locus of the proclamation, allowing religion to arrive without the requirement of deference to the originating culture. This we might call mission by *translation*, and it carries with it the need for indigenous theological inquiry, which arises as a necessary stage in the process of reception and adaptation."[12] Translation thus valorizes a distinctive language and culture so deeply that "it assumes a relative, secondary status for the culture of the message bearer."[13] When the Holy Spirit made Jesus's followers translators at Pentecost, God charted a course for the church that would respect as deeply as possible each language and culture into which Christianity would enter.

Many Cultures: The Gentile Breakthrough

As we've already seen, the stories of Babel and of Pentecost both begin with one community sharing a single common cultural identity. In both stories, that identity is marked primarily by a shared space and a shared language. In the case of Pentecost, Jesus's followers had gathered in one place, Jerusalem, and all speak one language, Aramaic. And, as we've already also seen, Jesus's Aramaic-speaking followers gathered in Jerusalem also share a common religious culture. They are devout Galilean

---

12. Sanneh, *Translating the Message*, 33–34.
13. Sanneh, *Translating the Message*, 34.

Jews, who had come to Jerusalem to celebrate one of Judaism's major festivals, Pentecost. In the first part of his story of Pentecost, Luke makes the particular Jewish roots of Christianity absolutely clear.

In the second part of his story, Luke continues to document Christianity's Jewish roots. The diverse members of the crowd gathered in Jerusalem for Pentecost, though from many different places and speaking many different languages, are themselves devout Jews (2:5). Furthermore, Luke tells us that when Jesus's followers leave Jerusalem to spread the message of Jesus throughout the world, they always begin to preach within the Jewish communities they encounter, and many Jews are persuaded by their message (Acts 11:19-21; 13:5, 14, 42; 14:1, etc.). But almost immediately, non-Jews are also attracted to the message of Jesus. The first and most prominent example is Cornelius, the Roman centurion stationed in Caesarea, whose whole family embraces the message of Jesus and is baptized (Acts 10). Peter, the Jewish missionary, must be shown by God directly in a vision (10:9-16) that, as Peter himself puts it, "God doesn't show partiality to one group of people over another" (10:34). The church would be a church of people from different places speaking different languages. And it would also be a church of people, not just from the Jewish background of Jesus's earliest followers but from different socioreligious backgrounds. It would move from its roots in Judaism to the variety of indigenous cultures that would embrace it.

Even though those present at Pentecost, representing the whole known world's countries and languages, were devout Jews, they also represent and anticipate the Gentile breakthrough, the fact that the church born at Pentecost would embrace people not just from its Jewish roots but from the entire diversity of the world's cultures and religions. Scholars are in wide agreement that by documenting the spread of Christianity from its source in Judaism to the wider non-Jewish world, Luke directed his work ultimately to Gentile Christians, like Theophilus, to whom he addresses both volumes of his account, and like himself, probably a Gentile convert to Judaism who became a Christian.[14] Luke's "leading purpose," as Richard Pervo states it, "is to demonstrate the legitimacy of the gentile mission."[15] From its single uniform cultural roots, the church explodes at Pentecost to embrace all the world's diversity: its lands, languages, and its Jewish and non-Jewish inhabitants alike.

Luke's charter for the church at Pentecost fits perfectly into his world-affirming perspective in the entirety of Luke-Acts. He constructs his whole narrative to place the church in the context of world history. Luke connects his story of Jesus and his followers to all humanity by tracing their heritage not just to Abraham, as does Matthew, but all the way back to the first human being, Adam (Luke 3:38). Furthermore, he grounds the events of Jesus's ministry and the early church in the political realities of the Roman Empire (Luke 2:1-2), an empire he values as providing the political orders that allow the church to spread. He shows respect for all, including those outside the Christian movement, as reasonable and open-minded people. All of this evidence points to the conclusion that Luke read the story of Babel with great generosity as an account of God's intention to create the diverse world in which he himself lived, and that he modeled on it the story of the church's birth at Pentecost, a church that God intended to mirror the world's diversity.

How Difference Became a Problem

As we've already seen, Christians from earliest times have seen Pentecost reversing Babel rather than building on it in a positive and constructive way, as Luke intended. They've read Pentecost

---

14. Luke Timothy Johnson, *The Gospel of Luke*, Sacra Pagina (Collegeville, MN: Liturgical Press, 1991), 9.

15. Pervo, *Acts*, 71.

as a story that aimed to correct what went wrong at Babel: the diversification of languages and the confusion, chaos, and violence that came of difference. Pentecost became a story of reunification, a story in which unity overcomes diversity, and a story in which oneness transcends difference. Oneness, not difference, became the theme of Pentecost. Transcending difference, not engaging and affirming difference, became Pentecost's definition of the church.

Pentecost's charter for the church became unity.

What happened? How did we build such a tenacious tradition of reading Pentecost as a story that transcends and overcomes difference rather than celebrates it, as Luke does? And why do we continue to preserve this way of reading the Pentecost story today? Why have Christians turned difference into a problem to be solved? The first reason is that we've inherited an interpretation of Luke's source for Pentecost, the Babel story, in which difference is, in fact, thought to be a problem. It is an interpretation that views the different cultures into which God divided the world as a punishment, a curse, and a disaster for the world. From earliest times, this reading became the dominant interpretation of Babel, as we've seen in chapter 1, and it has been nearly impossible to believe that Luke himself didn't read Babel in this way too. We've been locked into a reading of Babel that Luke wasn't locked into, a reading that disparaged difference as the source of confusion and conflict. And this has been the only starting point available for understanding Pentecost's relationship to Babel. Pentecost reversing Babel has been the only option. The alternative reading of Babel as a story that celebrates difference as God's intention for the world gives us a new—very old—starting point for understanding Luke's aims in his Pentecost story.

A second reason for reading Pentecost as a reversal of Babel is the common practice within Christianity of placing the New Testament over against the Old Testament. The relationship between the testaments, that is, the relationship between Christianity and its ancient Israelite and Jewish roots, has been conceived in a number of ways. The New Testament has been seen as the fulfillment of the Old Testament. The New Testament has been seen to be prefigured and foreshadowed by typologies or analogies with the Old Testament. And the New Testament has been seen as complementary or supplementary to the Old Testament as a witness to revelation. But perhaps the most popular way of viewing the relationship between the testaments has been to place the New Testament over against the Old Testament.

According to this view, the New Testament supersedes, makes obsolete, and even negates the Old Testament. The New Testament replaces the temporary and inadequate revelation of God in the Old Testament. Grace, for example, replaces law; the God of love replaces the God of wrath; forgiveness replaces judgment; faith replaces works. Using such a lens for reading the Old Testament story of Babel in relation to the New Testament story of Pentecost, it makes good sense to see Babel as a story of human sin and divine punishment overcome by the Christian experience of faith and empowerment by the Holy Spirit. The difference and chaos unleashed on the world at Babel is reversed by the unity of Pentecost. Our alternative reading of Babel as a story that celebrates difference as God's intention for the world, and the new understanding that Luke actually read the story in this way, reframes the Christian understanding of the relationship between the testaments in this case as one of continuity and complementarity. God's affirmation of difference at the world's beginning is renewed as God's intention for the church itself.

A third reason for reading Pentecost as a story that transcends and overcomes difference is the common understanding that early Christianity at its core was a movement that aimed to diminish and even eliminate ethnic differences. "Most historical reconstructions published in the last twenty years," writes Denise Buell, "depict earliest Christianity as an inclusive movement that rejected ethnic or racial specificity as a condition of religious identity."[16] Linked with this view, and related to the antithetical understanding of the testaments described above, is the Christian portrayal of Judaism as aggressively nationalistic and ethnocentric in contrast to a universal, ethnic-free Christianity. "In this way," writes Eric Barreto, "Christianity becomes an open association of all peoples wherein their differences are no longer of importance, in stark contrast to a purported Judaism with rigid lines of demarcation."[17] Pentecost reversing Babel fits perfectly into this perception of Christianity. Pentecost shows a church moving beyond the dangerous differences introduced at Babel. Pentecost's main theme in this logic becomes unity, universalism, and oneness.

One crucial part of this idea that Pentecost reverses Babel is the idea of "confusion." As we've seen in chapter 1, translators, without merit in the Hebrew text itself, have rendered God's mixing or multiplication of the world's languages at Babel with the word *confusion*, a term implying misunderstanding, chaos, and conflict. "Come, let us go down, and confuse their language" (Gen 11:7, 9 NRSV). This translation was fatal. It disparaged multilingualism at Babel, and it continues to infect the reading of the Pentecost story. There, the crowd's response to the multilingualism they heard is often compared to Babel's confusion, especially at the very end of the story, when some jeered at what they didn't understand, saying, "They're full of new wine" (Acts 2:13). "This," writes Pervo, "is a confusion worthy of Babel."[18] And he goes on to call what happened at Pentecost "a utopian restoration of the unity of the human race."[19] In fact, different languages are different and not understood by all. This is a simple hallmark of difference. It was true at Babel, when the Storyteller says, "they won't understand each other's language" (Gen 11:7).

16. Denise Kimber Buell, "Rethinking the Relevance of Race for Early Christian Self-Definition," *Harvard Theological Review* 94 (2001): 453.
17. Barreto, "Negotiating Difference," 130.
18. Pervo, *Acts*, 59.
19. Pervo, *Acts*, 61–62.

And it is true at Pentecost, when Luke says, "They were mystified because everyone heard them speaking in their native languages" (Acts 2:6). The different languages at Pentecost are not a distant reflection of Babel's confusion to be overcome. At both Babel and Pentecost they are simply different languages. And they are the hallmark of the church.

Finally, we must reckon with one more reason for our own acceptance of this reading of Pentecost as a reversal of Babel rather than an affirmation of its diversity. That is our own discomfort with difference. We find it hard to believe, as Chimamanda Adichie says, that difference is ordinary, is normal, is the reality of our world. We find it hard to believe, as Eric Barreto says, that human differences are "theologically vibrant sites for God's actions in the world." We may hope for a world in which ethnic conflict ceases to exist, but to deny the importance of ethnic identity and the reality of difference eventually leads to a refusal to live with it. Luke was a courageous Christian with a courageous charter for the church. He was willing not only to acknowledge ethnic identity and difference but to see it as the hallmark of the church of which he was a member.

Reading Pentecost Today

Luke's story of the church's charter at Pentecost remains strikingly contemporary and real for Christians today. The Pentecost story engages the most basic issues about identity and difference the church has faced through its history. Those issues are as strong and specific today as they have ever been. Christians around the world continue to deal with the legacy of Western colonialism and the missionary movement that accompanied it, which attempted to impose a single cultural identity on the diverse ethnicities it encountered, thereby destroying the self-respect and integrity of indigenous cultures. In the United States, old denominational identities of the church are eroding and new movements are arising. Racial and ethnic differences continue to divide the larger church, in which the hour of worship on Sunday morning remains the most segregated hour of the week, as Dr. Martin Luther King Jr. reminded and admonished Christians.

One of the most striking and important experiences I've had teaching and learning with students at McCormick Theological Seminary is talking with first-year students who are encountering Christians different from themselves for the first time in their lives. The denominational, ethnic, racial, and international diversity at McCormick means that even in a single small group of eight to ten first-year students within our entry course, each person has different beliefs and practices about what it is to be a Christian. For them to discover devout Christians who are different from themselves is surprising and a little bewildering. It also changes them. Encountering difference inevitably turns out to be a deeply broadening experience, an experience that grows and enriches their view of the church. I am reminded daily, even in the small neighborhood of Hyde Park and the slightly larger neighborhood of South Chicago where McCormick is located, how much difference is a hallmark of the church and how much recognizing and engaging it directly forms our students into more broadminded and compassionate people.

When read in its traditional way as a reversal of Babel, the story of Pentecost reinforces our suspicions about difference and our wish to transcend and move beyond it. According to this reading, the story of Pentecost buys into the old understanding of Babel that difference is dangerous. It continues to teach us that God's introduction of difference at Babel was God's punishment on the world and the origin of confusion, chaos, and conflict. It continues to feed our suspicion and fear of difference. Read in its traditional way as a reversal of Babel and a restoration of unity, Pentecost changes nothing. Difference is still a problem. Difference is regarded not as the hallmark of the church embedded in the church's charter, but as a source of confusion to be transcended and overcome in the new Christian movement. This is a perilous place to begin thinking about difference and living with it in the church.

Rereading the story of Pentecost can open our eyes to this story's celebration of difference as a hallmark of Christianity. It can also open our eyes to our comfortable acceptance of the negative understanding of difference embedded in our traditional reading. Rereading the story of Pentecost as a story that acknowledges and embraces both ethnic identity and ethnic difference gives us a new—really, very old—and positive starting point for thinking about difference in the church. Not only does it give us an opportunity to reexamine the negative attitudes toward difference that have governed our traditional reading of this story, but it also provides a starting point for developing new and constructive views for thinking about and living with difference in the church today.

The story of Pentecost, reread, can do this for us in two important ways. First, the story of Pentecost recognizes the reality of and declares the importance of ethnic identity as a cornerstone of Christian identity. Luke builds the value of cultural distinctiveness into the church's charter. Just as the Storyteller in Genesis recognized the reality and value of constructing a distinctive identity by the world's first people (Gen 11:1-4), so Luke recognizes the reality and value of distinctive cultural identities for the church. He does so, in the first place, by acknowledging the origin of Christianity in the small distinctive community of Aramaic-speaking Galilean Jews who followed Jesus gathered in Jerusalem. He further emphasizes the ethnic particularity of Christian origins by making the devout diaspora Jews in Jerusalem the first hearers of the Pentecost message (Acts 2:5), by identifying the Jewish communities outside of Jerusalem as the first audience to hear the gospel message, by emphasizing the numbers of Jews who responded to the message (21:20), and by affirming the Jewish heritage and perspective as an ongoing aspect of the church's identity.

And Luke's Pentecost story doesn't value the church's distinctive culture of origin alone. It values just as highly the myriad ethnicities into whose languages the message of Jesus is translated at Pentecost. Each distinctive ethnicity becomes a legitimate home and habitation of Christianity, a place where Christianity will flourish within its own unique concepts and practices. No single culture will corner the gospel message. This *translatability* of the gospel into different languages, the primary theme of Luke's Pentecost story, is, as Lamin Sanneh has shown us, Christianity's crucial move to honor ethnic identity and indigenous cultures. Placing the message of Jesus into the hands of an indigenous community and its native speakers makes them the experts in articulating the message and empowers them to determine its proper modes of cultural expression. Among the consequences of scriptural translatability and its ethnic empowerment Sanneh counts "cultural self-understanding, vernacular pride, social awakening, religious renewal, cross-cultural dialogue, transmission and recipiency, [and] reciprocity in mission."[20] The translatability of the message embedded in the church's charter at Pentecost ensures the integrity of each ethnic identity itself as a hallmark of Christianity. On the basis of Luke's Pentecost story, we could say *the* hallmark.

The church has a history of epic failures, of course, to follow through on its commitment to ethnic integrity and difference in its charter at Pentecost. Repeatedly, a particular cultural embodiment of Christianity has taken itself to be the normative and absolute expression of Jesus's message, to which all other ethnic identities must conform. This issue arose at the church's very beginning when some members of the Jerusalem church argued that all Christian converts adopt the full range of the religious practices of the Jewish culture out of which Christianity arose. Ultimately, the Jerusalem Council firmly rejected this demand

20. Sanneh, *Translating the Message*, 2.

for cultural exclusivity and hegemony (Acts 15:1-35), though debates about this continued. Soon afterward the synthesis between Christianity and the Hellenistic culture, into which Christianity first moved from its Jewish roots, hardened into a cultural arrogance that became the rule for others.

The main and most virulent modern manifestation of this impulse to absolutize one ethnic expression of Christianity over others is the church's role as a partner in Western colonialism. In the United States, white Christian colonialists from Europe have demonized and destroyed Native American cultures, dehumanized and enslaved African cultures, and obstructed and harassed immigrant communities from other parts of the world. Around the globe, Western colonialism has imposed its own form of cultural Christianity on countless indigenous cultures, destroying their identity and integrity.

As a constant challenge to this cultural arrogance that has so frequently gripped Christianity is the translatability of the gospel at Pentecost, which honors every ethnicity in its own language and on its own terms as the legitimate home of the gospel message and of Christianity. Translation, as we have seen, assumes the integrity and expertise of the host language and culture, and by doing so it relativizes the culture of the message bearer and translator. It reveals the originating language and culture as ultimately inadequate and ineffective for the shaping of the gospel in its new culture. By honoring the indigenous culture into which the gospel is translated and relativizing the normative status of the translator's culture, Christianity is always at heart radically pluralistic—as radically pluralistic as the first hearers at Pentecost.

Here is the power of translation for the church, first experienced at Pentecost, as Sanneh describes it:

> The emergence of non-Western languages and culture was a significant victory for history's underdogs, and equally for the prospects of intercultural solidarity. Few things have done more to mitigate the dialectic of power and injustice than confidence in a God who

looks kindly on identity of tongue and soil. We can overcome barriers of exclusion and suspicion only when we turn to the one God in our own idiom, for that idiom in its variety is what we all have in common as the ground of our concrete individuality. It is there that God will meet and not leave us. As long as we accept the need to translate, the stream of a universal providence will continue to swell with the outpourings of a variegated humanity in its open, inclusive form.[21]

By honoring each distinctive culture and its native language as the authentic home of the gospel, Pentecost embraces difference without qualification. It provided the starting point for thinking about and living with difference in the church in Luke's day, and it still provides a sound starting point for living with difference in the church today. Luke embraces difference, as does the Babel narrative, as God's work. As God created the multiple cultures of Luke's world at the beginning of time (Gen 11:1-9), so the Holy Spirit invited all those cultures into the church by the miracle of multilingualism at Pentecost. Just as God made difference normal as the reality of the world, so the Holy Spirit made difference normal as the reality of the church.

When the Holy Spirit embraces each culture as an authentic part of Christianity at Pentecost, God grants each culture equal worth. God recognizes no culture as the dominant or normative measure of Christian identity, not even the culture of Christianity's origins. God stigmatizes no culture's difference as deficient. And God excludes no culture from the church. Such an image of the church's radical pluralism guards against the fear and suspicion of difference. Such an absolute valuation of multiple ethnic identities counters the tensions, prejudice, and conflict that difference can provoke. The continuous translatability of the message makes difference the hallmark of the church.

Identity and difference. Luke, just as the Storyteller of Babel in Genesis 11, places them side by side in his account of the

21. Sanneh, *Translating the Message*, 8.

church's charter at Pentecost in order to say that both are real and normal. Both define human experience. Both are part of the world God made and the church God created at Pentecost. This is a revolutionary way of reading the story of Babel and a revolutionary way of reading the story of Pentecost. And it can be a revolutionary way of thinking about difference and living with it today.

Conclusion

New Conversations
about Difference

*Don't ignore color or gender—that's ignoring my identity. Let's celebrate
those things and let's celebrate those differences.*

—Michael Atkins, Principal of Stedman Elementary School, Denver
Public School System[1]

T his book opens up a new conversation with the book
of Genesis about difference. Moments of crisis, like today's particular and potent social conflicts and divisions,
throw us back on our founding documents and on the ultimate
sources of our thought and values for reorientation to the world.
The Bible, and the book of Genesis in particular, is the bedrock
of these sources. For all those where Judaism, Christianity, and
Islam have taken root and for Western civilization itself, Genesis
contains the founding stories that define culture, that shape its
thought, and that found its values. These stories established in
their own ways the world in which we live. They provide the para-
digms for our imaginations. They continue to influence in conscious and unconscious ways how we think and act. It is essential

1. Scottie Andrew and Brian Ries, "He Started as a Custodian. Now He's a Principal in the Same School District," CNN, June 11, 2019, www.msn.com/en-us/news
/good-news/he-started-as-a-custodian-now-hes-a-principal-in-the-same-school-district
/ar-AACInms?ocid=spartandhp.

that we become aware of the way that they have shaped us. We must also understand their power to move us toward constructive or destructive responses to cultural difference.

The book of Genesis is a uniquely powerful treatise on cultural identity and cultural difference. In its genealogies and genealogical narratives, its authors write to articulate their own identity in the world and to locate themselves within the vast array of identities of others, reflecting continually on their relationship with others in their world of difference. Constructing identity and negotiating difference are as old as the earliest human relationships. The values in these stories are as important as they ever were, and they wield great power.

To open up a new and authentic conversation with the book of Genesis about difference, we've had to acknowledge the long and powerful tradition of Genesis's interpreters, many of whom have read its stories through lenses that view difference as a danger and that exclude and devalue others. This move by interpreters toward more negative readings of biblical stories is a phenomenon that scholars have noticed in various forms. James Kugel talks about "the polarization that takes place in ancient exegesis," by which Israel's ancestors are viewed as entirely good, while others are altogether demonized.[2] Ron Hendel describes the treatment of Balaam over time, whose early image as a virtuous foreign seer is transformed into an agent of sin.[3] We've seen this tendency in various guises in the chapters of this book. In the way interpreters since the author of *Jubilees* have turned identity-building into arrogance and cultural difference into punishment in the story of Babel. In the way interpreters turned all members of Noah's descendants except for Abraham's lineage into sinners outside the realm of God's care. These are interpretive readings of binary imaginations that turn the world simplistically into "us" and

---

2. James L. Kugel, *The Bible As It Was* (Cambridge, MA: Harvard University Press, 1997), 27.

3. Ronald Hendel, *Remembering Abraham: Culture, Memory, and History in the Hebrew Bible* (Oxford: Oxford University Press, 2005), 3–7.

"them," that exaggerate differences and divide peoples, that lump and stereotype "them" into a falsely homogeneous group, that turn others into a single Other, who, as Jonathan Z. Smith points out, is considered unintelligible and impossible to engage.[4]

These interpretive lenses are, regrettably, the lenses we've been given to read Genesis. As James Kugel reminds us, it's this interpreted Bible, rather than the actual Bible on the page, that we carry with us in our minds and that continues to influence us.[5] So we've assimilated an interpretation of Genesis that's viewed difference as a threat more than an opportunity, that's viewed others through an exclusionary lens, and that's imagined them as less righteous or less blessed or less than fully human. It is these lenses that have masked the true views of identity and difference held by the writers of Genesis. It is these lenses that we have worked to cast aside in the reading of Genesis above. It is only by this effort to set aside these traditional and dysfunctional lenses that we've been able to recover the authentic views of Genesis about identity and difference.

Having set aside these lenses, we've been able to read stories in Genesis that we thought we already knew in a new way. We've been able to hear the genuine voices of Genesis's authors and to encounter the actual imaginations by which they engaged difference. Entirely new conversations with Genesis are now possible. And these conversations have major consequences for thinking about difference. They had major consequences in their authors' own worlds, and they have major consequences for thinking about difference and living with it today. Each chapter of this book has opened up a new conversation with Genesis about difference entirely impossible within the old lenses that viewed difference as a threat.

---

4. Jonathan Z. Smith, "Differential Equations: On Constructing the 'Other'" (Thirteenth Annual University Lecture in Religion, Arizona State University, Tempe, AZ, March 5, 1992).

5. Kugel, *The Bible as It Was*, 1–49.

These new conversations with Genesis help us rediscover its core perspectives on difference that we can summarize now. They are the foundational perspectives on difference held by Genesis's authors that the old lenses have hidden from us.

The first of these core values is that difference is normal. Difference is the reality we all share and the reality we all start from. It's the reality that we all have in common. Put in the theological terms of Genesis's authors, difference is God's intention for the world. It's the world God wanted and the world God wanted people to live in. That is the point when the Storyteller attributes to God the creation of the world's diverse cultures in the story of Babel. That is the point when Genesis's authors explain the real and legitimate spaces in their world occupied by their Ishmaelite and Edomite neighbors, and the real and legitimate spaces occupied in their own ethnic group by its various tribes descended from Jacob's sons. That is the point when Luke describes the birth of the church as a multilingual event. Claiming that difference is God's decision for the world and claiming that all its peoples have God-given spaces in that world is the theological foundation of difference in the book of Genesis and in the account of Pentecost that draws from it.

The second core value is that difference is always viewed within a network of relatedness. Difference is not a random distribution of disconnected peoples and isolated ethnicities. This idea of relatedness is grounded in Genesis's authors' own social experience of kinship and in their use of kinship language to explain their own identity and their relationship to others. In a world imagined from the perspective of kinship, others are never autonomous. Their difference never detaches them, isolates them, and cuts them loose from a connection with others. Others are always imagined as part of a kinship network. They are all relatives. This imagination provides the basis for claiming connections and building bridges. It embraces others and provides a starting point for understanding the common humanity everyone shares. We've seen this core value foundationally in Genesis's authors' claim that Israel belongs to the great family tree descended from its founding ancestor Noah. We've seen it in Genesis's authors' careful explanations of their family connections to their closest neighbors the Ishmaelites and Edomites. We've seen it even in their construction of Israel's own ethnic identity when Genesis's authors affirm the family relationship of the discrete tribes that David gathered to form the kingdom of Israel, all presented as descendants of each of Jacob's twelve sons.

The third core value about identity and difference is an imagination big enough to combine realism, generosity, and optimism about living with difference. Genesis's authors do not deny the conflict that differences can ignite. They recognize the potential for distrust, distancing, and violence when difference is encountered. And they even entertain the idea that such conflict can end it all. It can erase others. They are realists. But they are not pessimists. They construct narratives not to deny conflict, to decry conflict, or to surrender to it. They construct narratives to explore conflict and to plot ways through it. Their descriptions of conflict are never simplistic. They recognize the complex nature of conflict and the complicated investment in it of those involved. They reject a binary imagination of "us" and "them."

Above all, Genesis's authors plot a way forward through conflict toward a new future. To do so, they possess two great powers. On the one hand, they value deeply the importance of belonging and they take pride in their own identity. On the other, they have developed the breadth of mind to imagine the experience of others. Their stories are constructed so that all characters are real characters with human breadth and depth, both those characters who are members of their lineage and those who are members of other lineages. They can even imagine the compassionate generosity of others. They place all characters under the care of God. Ultimately, their stories plot a way through conflict by which differences can flourish. Israel's ancestors and others share in God's care within the diverse world God brought into being. Pentecost plots a future for the church in which all lands and languages have a place.

Difference is not benign. It is full of power to tear down and to build up. To destroy and to create. To end life and to bear new life. New conversations about difference are as crucial today as they have ever been. This is true in each of the worlds, big and small, that we inhabit. It is true in the world of Michael Atkins, whose words I've quoted at the beginning of this chapter because they so strikingly capture the ancient values of Genesis. When he was bused from his predominantly black neighborhood to a predominantly white middle school as a desegregation initiative, he experienced clear differences in how teachers treated students based on race. When later in life he applied to be a teacher's aide, he was offered a custodial position instead. After gaining his degree and certification, he became a teacher, an assistant principal, and now principal of Stedman Elementary School in Denver, Colorado, in the same school district where he was once a custodian. As principal, he is working to end the racial disparities he experienced as a student, bridge racial and cultural divides, and inspire students to embrace each other's differences. "I have an opportunity to do diversity right," he told CNN. And he describes his vision with values that reflect the same values we've seen in the ancient stories in Genesis, a respect for ethnic identity and an embrace of difference. "Don't ignore color or gender—that's ignoring my identity. Let's celebrate those things and let's celebrate those differences."[6]

We all live in such real communities and social contexts, where living with difference is an urgent challenge and where discovering how to celebrate differences will determine the quality of our future. The stakes are as high as they have ever been.

---

6. Andrew and Ries, "He Started as a Custodian."